Where
was God on
September 11?

Where was God on September 11?

Seeds of Faith and Hope

Edited by
Donald B. Kraybill and
Linda Gehman Peachey

Herald
Press

Scottdale, Pennsylvania
Waterloo, Ontario

Library of Congress Cataloging-in-Publication Data
Where was God on September 11? : seeds of faith and hope / edited by
Donald B. Kraybill and Linda Gehman Peachey.
    p. cm.
Includes bibliographical references.
ISBN 0-8361-9214-1 (pbk. : alk. paper)
1. September 11 Terrorist Attacks, 2001. 2. Terrorism—Religious aspects—
    Christianity. I. Kraybill, Donald B. II. Peachey, Linda Gehman.
BT736.15 .W46 2002
242'.4—dc21   2001007108

The paper used in this publication is recycled and meets the minimum requirements of American National Standard for Information Sciences—Permanence of
Paper for Printed Library Materials, ANSI Z39.48-1984.

WHERE WAS GOD ON SEPTEMBER 11?
Copyright © 2002 by Herald Press, Scottdale, Pa. 15683
    Published simultaneously in Canada by Herald Press,
    Waterloo, Ont. N2L 6H7. All rights reserved
Library of Congress Control Number: 2001007108
International Standard Book Number: 0-8361-9214-1
Design: book, Jim Butti; cover, Merrill Miller; photo of WTC, Getty Images/
    Peter Morgan; of daisy, Jim Bishop. Printed in the United States of
    America
11 10 09 08 07 06 05 04 03 02 10 9 8 7 6 5 4 3 2
To order or request information, please call 1-800-759-4447 (individuals);
1-800-245-7894 (trade). Website: www.mph.org

Our Refuge and Strength

God is our refuge and strength,
    a very present help in trouble.
Therefore we will not fear,
      though the earth should change,
      though the mountains shake in the heart of the sea;
      though its waters roar and foam,
      though the mountains tremble with its tumult.

The nations are in an uproar, the kingdoms totter;
    he utters his voice, the earth melts.
The Lord of hosts is with us;
    the God of Jacob is our refuge.

Come, behold the works of the LORD;
    see what desolations he has brought on the earth.
He makes wars cease to the end of the earth;
    he breaks the bow, and shatters the spear;
    he burns the shields with fire.

"Be still, and know that I am God!
    I am exalted among the nations,
    I am exalted in the earth."
The Lord of hosts is with us;
    the God of Jacob is our refuge.

—*Excerpted from Psalm 46*

Contents

Faith in the Face of Terror

September 11, 2001, has become a national symbol of terror and tragedy. The horrific events of that day stirred a new search for answers to many profound religious questions. What drives the human heart to evil? How can people be so malicious? Why do bad things happen to good people? Can people of faith support retaliation? And most troubling of all, where was God in all of this?

These age-old questions suddenly loomed anew as destruction struck New York, Pennsylvania, and Washington, D.C., by surprise, and as the aftershocks rumbled around the world. The wrenching questions came into even sharper focus as bombs began dropping in Afghanistan and the fear of anthrax stalked America.

These events also brought a great outpouring of love as hundreds, yes, millions of people, responded with generosity and heroic acts of love. Black and white, Republican and Democrat, rich and poor, Muslim and Christian—so many people joined together to help victims at home and abroad. Old boundaries and labels vanished as people of all stripes reached out to care for those in need. In a short sliver of time, we saw the devastating depths of evil and the magnificent heights of love—a dramatic contrast of malice and goodness. We saw the worst and the best of the human community.

How can people of faith make sense of these events? What do the events of September 11 teach us about God, good, evil, love, forgiveness, and justice? Are there other ways to respond to these events beyond the stark choice of despair and retaliation?

The essays in this volume chronicle stories of faith as people struggle with these difficult questions and search for meaning amid the tragedy of terror. Many people, understandably, swelled with anger and rage. Some hungered for retaliation; others were paralyzed with fear. These essays offer a third track, another way of responding, a search for nonviolent alternatives in the midst of rage and despair.

We have called these essays "seeds of faith and hope" because they offer the promise of a better world. They bring suggestions that we hope will sprout from the rubble and grow into peaceful solutions. The entries in this journal of faith, crafted in the tumultuous wake of September 11, do not offer complex peace-building proposals. The writers are primarily religious people, not policy analysts. The entries, however, carry seeds of hope for people of faith as they walk through the valley of the shadow of fear. From a variety of theological perspectives, many of the essays explore nonviolent alternatives to military action.

Most of the entries have been adapted from longer texts of sermons, letters, or essays that appeared elsewhere, with due care to preserve the writers' meanings. We scanned a wide array of materials and selected those that spoke to us in special ways. Due to space limitations, we regretfully had to leave out much good material.

The authors do not necessarily agree with each other, nor do we agree with all of them. But they have helpful words for people of faith in the wake of September 11. Most important, they speak words of healing, hope, and care.

This is not an ordinary book, but then the fall of 2001 was not an ordinary time. The essays do not fall neatly into tidy chapters like an ordinary book. The boundaries between chapters are fluid and often overlapping. We see the pieces as entries in a journal of faith. Some are long and others are mere snippets, but together they chronicle stories of faith in the face of terror.

We owe a bundle of gratitude to many friends who nurtured these stories into print in a short period of time. First, we acknowledge the generosity of the authors, who granted us permission to adapt and use their work. We especially thank Edgar Stoesz for voicing the vision for a collection of essays that would chronicle the religious questions flowing from September 11.

Others who provided support and suggestions include John Bomberger, Cathleen Hockman-Wert, Michael King, Susan Mark Landis, John A. Lapp, Titus Peachey, and Norman Shenk. We also thank Terri Hopkins, Mark Lacher, and Angie Wagner for superb support with word processing, editing, and other tasks.

We could not have dreamed of better support from our publisher, Herald Press. Levi Miller and David Garber gave unwavering attention and priority to this project at every turn. Along with their larger team, they turned our manuscript into a book in an incredibly short time.

Finally, we thank several anonymous donors who provided financial assistance to underwrite the project.

More than eighty days have passed since jetliners exploded into the twin towers of the World Trade Center. The smoke still rises from the pile of rubble and destruction. And the dust still flies in Afghanistan as the smart bombs strike their targets. Amid the anger, pain, and destruction, we offer these seeds of faith and hope—hope for a better and more peaceful world for our children and theirs to come.

Chapter 1

God Amid the Terror?

The destruction on September 11 exposed the anger lurking in the recesses of the human heart. Thousands of innocent people, caught by surprise, were crushed and burned alive. The attack was calculated, cold, and cruel. The subsequent bombings in Afghanistan brought another wave of devastation to thousands of people there.

Terror filled the air at home and abroad. The excruciating torment led some to echo the cry of Jesus from the cross, "My God, my God, why have you forsaken me?" For others, in the weeks following the attack, God became an abiding refuge in the storm of terror as they sought sanctuary in churches, temples, mosques, and synagogues.

The tragedy brought a great outpouring of love from the human heart as hundreds and even millions of people responded with generosity. In some cases, heroic acts of love led to their death. What motivated the millions of people to make generous donations of time, blood, food, money, and many other gifts? And in Afghanistan and nearby countries, what drove aid workers and local citizens to care for the hungry and wounded, fighting for life in the crossfire of war?

Where was God amid of all the tragedy and suffering? The essays in chapter 1 probe this question from a variety of perspectives—seeking answers, in these times, to age-old issues.

Where Was God?

John P. Braun

Where was God when the twin towers fell and the Pentagon burned? Where is God when terror seems to have the upper hand? Where is God when everything we have ever trusted in is caving in around us? I believe that when our trust in the false gods of violence, security, wealth, and power collapse or blow apart, God is among us, offering us a faith in the One in whom all things hold together.

The psalmist writes, "I call upon God, and the LORD will save me" (Ps. 55:16). We need salvation now from the terror within us and from the terror that we are so willing to pass on to others. God calls us to be saved from our trust in the power of wealth. God calls us to be saved from our trust in the terror of violence. As Christians, God calls us to find salvation through our trust in Christ. The writer of Proverbs (18:10) says, "The name of the Lord is a strong tower; the righteous run into it and are safe."

Where is God in all of this? I believe that God is there when people feel and practice compassion for those who suffer. We have witnessed this in New York. In the story of Matthew 25, the nations are gathered together for judgment. The great Judge says,

> Come, . . . inherit the kingdom prepared for you from the foundation of the world; for I was hungry and you gave me food, I was thirsty and you gave me something to drink, I was a stranger and you welcomed me, I was

naked and you gave me clothing, I was sick and you took care of me, I was in prison and you visited me. . . . As you did it to one of the least of these who are members of my family, you did it to me. (Matt. 25:34-40)

Where is God in all of this? God is among those who are suffering and hurting and grieving. God is in those who are now being terrorized, wherever they may be. God is in those Arab countries that are now terrorized by the fearsome thought of being attacked by the most powerful military force on earth. God is in the hearts of the New Yorkers whose lives have been altered. God is there, in all such scenes.

While we reach out as followers of Christ to heal, to comfort, to feed, to visit, and so on, we are meeting God in those situations. Where is God in all of this? God is there when people mourn. Jesus says, "Blessed are those who mourn, for they will be comforted. . . . Blessed are the pure in heart, for they will see God" (Matt. 5:4, 8).

The way of terror takes us from grief to anger, to hatred. It eats us up alive, and perhaps that is the most terrible thing. But God is with people who mourn and seeks to bless them, sometimes through us. Mourning in the presence of God can have a purifying effect on us, and Jesus promises that the pure in heart will see God.

As followers of Jesus, we are called to witness and observe the times in which we live. We are called to use the teachings of Jesus to make sense out of the things that happen in our lives. And we are called to practice the teachings of Jesus as the way of salvation.

We are not helpless. We are children of God. Life is not hopeless. Our hope is in Christ. Fear need not consume us, because love casts out fear and covers a multitude of sins (cf. 1 John 4:18; 1 Pet. 4:8).

We will not worship terror and retaliation. We worship the God who is revealed in Jesus Christ and is with us through the Holy Spirit. Amen.

John P. Braun pastors Charleswood Mennonite Church, Winnipeg, Manitoba. Adapted from a sermon, September 16, 2001.

Where Was God on 9/11?

Philip Yancey

The phones started ringing at our house on the day of the attack. I took calls from England, Holland, and Australia, as well as the U.S. media. "You've written about the problem of pain. What do you have to say about this tragedy?" In truth, I had nothing to say. The facts were so overpowering, so incomprehensible, that I was stunned into silence. Anything I could think of saying— "Horrible. Don't blame God. The face of evil"—sounded like a cliché. In every case, I declined to respond. Like most Americans, I felt unbearably helpless, wounded, and deeply sad.

Wednesday, the day after the attacks, it dawned on me that I had already presented much of what I believe about the problem of pain. I wrote *Where Is God When It Hurts?* in 1977 as a 28-year-old who had no right to tackle questions of theodicy—and also no ability to resist. There is no more urgent question facing those of us who identify ourselves as Christian. In 1990, I revised the book, adding about a hundred pages and the perspective of middle age.

Where is God in the midst of this? Recently, in Washington and Chicago, as I talked about the special edition of *Where Is God When It Hurts?* interviewers would turn the question back on me. "Well, where is God at a time like this?" Sometimes I countered some of the harmful things other Christian spokesmen had said, bringing guilt and judgment to a time that begged for comfort and grace. I talked of Jesus' response to tragedies, especially in Luke 13.

Then I told of a man who came up to me one time and said, "Sorry, I don't have time to read your book. Can you just answer that question for me in a sentence or two?"

I thought for a moment and said, "I guess the answer to that question is another question: 'Where is the church when it hurts?' If the church is doing its job—binding up wounds, comforting the grieving, offering food to the hungry—I don't think people will wonder so much where God is when it hurts. They'll know where God is: in the presence of his people on earth."

We also learned that love for country and even for strangers can surge up with no warning. We learned that our nation, for all its flaws, has much worth preserving and worth defending. And we learned that at a time of crisis, we turn to our spiritual roots: the U.S. president quoting Psalm 23, the bagpiper piping "Amazing Grace," the sanitation workers stopping by their makeshift chapel, the Salvation Army chaplains dispensing grace, the pastors comforting the grieving loved ones. Thanks to them, we know where God is when it hurts.

Philip Yancey is author of Where Is God When It Hurts? *Adapted from a longer essay in* Christianity Today on-line.

My God, Why Have You Forsaken Me?

George Williamson Jr.

"My God, it's falling!" is what I said. I'm into tall buildings. Their majesty snatches up my imagination and charges the blood. The World Trade towers especially, dwarfing lower Manhattan—the most exciting cityscape on earth—with ultimate images of solidity, hugeness, and human self-transcendence. Incredibly, hysterically, we watched both towers implode, crumbling to the earth as a pile of rubble, in glass, steel, and concrete fragments.

Thousands of people inside, their lives twisted and crushed out before our very eyes. "My God!" Civilians the target, civilians the weapon! "My God!" This is absolutely unthinkable, unspeakable, too terrible for words. The only words I've found for it are these: "My God!" "My God, my God, why have you forsaken me?"

We had to watch it throughout the day, throughout the week. I tried to stop watching, but I couldn't snatch my eyes away. Then we learned that among the thousands crushed by the toppling giants were more than two hundred firefighters and fifty police officers who were performing heroic rescues.

Later I heard two stories about the rescuers. One came from an Episcopal priest friend to whom one of the firefighters came before going downtown, asking him to hear his confession, just in case. . . .

The other came from my New York daughter. It was a drawing she saw, the silhouette of twin figures, a firefighter and a police officer, standing together atop the rubble. The caption, "The Twin Towers." Civilians the target. Civilians the weapon. My God!

On the cross Jesus cries out with Psalm 22, "My God, my God, why have you forsaken me?" (Mark 15:34). Jesus—the absolutely unthinkable happening, life draining from his crucified body, death now just hours away. "My God!" He quotes Psalm 22, an old war song from the Hebrew Psalter:

> My God, my God, why have you forsaken me?
> > Why are you so far from helping me,
> > > from the words of my groaning?
> O my God, I cry by day, but you do not answer;
> > and by night, but find no rest. (Ps. 22:1-2)

Hanging on the cross and looking down at the dancing mob laughing, shaking their fists at him, and taunting the disaster befalling him, Jesus thinks of Psalm 22. At that moment, crying out these ancient words, I want you to imagine Jesus feeling the force of their hatred. Jesus was human, like us. He had ordinary human feelings, like ours.

We are dealing with these very feelings. There's the horror, the rage, the numbing grief at this unthinkable and unprecedented and utterly demonic act, the vast sympathy for the victims, the deep hurt for New York City, the grief and love for our country.

Psalm 22 is a war song, written by and for a people at war. On other days I find that I am offended by the themes of these biblical war songs. But not today. I confess to having been perplexed at Jesus for choosing a war song for his final hymn on the day of his crucifixion. But not today. For good or ill, our president and 90 percent of those polled say we are at war. And Jesus too went down under terrorist attack.

So today, with Jesus, with the warrior poets of ancient Israel, I'm glad these words voice the unspeakable "My God!" for the godforsaken—words of terror for those under terrorist attack, words that are prayers to God. In this poem I'm astonished when, sharply and surprisingly, it turns to say, in effect, "In the dawning new day we now begin to praise the Lord for deliverance" (Ps. 22:22-31; cf. 46:5). So I recommit myself to the theological point of view!

Therefore, I shall not be just a militant realist, meeting violent force with yet more violent force. I shall not be simply a patriotic American, drawn in merely to the narrow interests of my country and its economy. That view, which dominated the world that ended on September 11, has failed.

Henceforth, I shall think with the mind of God as my mentor. And God is love (1 John 4:8). God's only purpose is peace. Psalm 22, a war song, is perhaps the most dreadful of all the Psalms. My God! The following Psalm is also a war song, too, but it strikes another mood. You know what it is: "The Lord is my shepherd, I shall not want." It's a soldier's song, boasting of his God: "You prepare a table before me in the presence of my enemies."

So look! Even though something has gone horribly wrong, the Lord is my shepherd. Even though God-fanatics from across the world believe God commanded them to suicide attack my institutions and me, the Lord is my shepherd, too. Even though people around the world with whom I identify, whose cause I support, dance in the street at my downfall,

The Lord is my shepherd, I shall not want.
God makes me lie down in green pastures.
God leads me beside still waters.
God restores my soul. (Ps. 23:1-2, adapted)

The poem's image amid the battle is not of a surprising new weapon, an unexpected victory, or a special set of armor. It is a table, prepared before me, in the presence of my enemies. A table! So God, whom some around the world believe to have ordered divine judgment against me, has said to me, "I am your God, your shepherd, too. And God has taken the gifts given me, and with them has set up a feast in the battlefield. And there it is, the twin invitation, to me and to my enemy, to sit down and have table fellowship."

Psalm 23 was set in the book of Psalms after the dreadful Psalm 22. It was meant to be set there, meant to be read as we have read it, after we have cried out, "My God!" And confessed this terrible godforsakenness. And moaned at the multiform terrorist attack upon us. Then we learn that God is our shepherd, and that we shall not want. That God anoints our wounded head with oil, and pours out cups of water, in our behalf, for the rescue workers at ground zero.

And "even though I walk through the valley of the shadow of death," through the urban caverns beneath the billowing clouds of death, "I will fear no evil, for you are with me. Your rod and your staff, they comfort me. . . ."

"Surely goodness and mercy shall follow me" in the new world coming. And I shall maintain my hold on the mind of God "forever" (cf. Ps. 23:4, 6, KJV). Amen.

George Williamson Jr. is Senior Pastor at First Baptist Church, Granville, Ohio. Adapted from a sermon, September 16, 2001.

United in a New Kind of Grief

Peter Eaton

How should people of faith respond to terrorism? The three historic religious traditions of Judaism, Islam, and Christianity share a noble heritage. Not only are our origins bound up with one another, not only do we claim a common ancestry in our father Abraham, we also we share a common destiny. For we know that until there is genuine peace and justice between Christian, Jew, and Muslim, there will be no peace and justice on earth. We speak a language about God that is not about hate, and we must speak that common language of faith clearly now more than ever.

First and foremost, this terrible and horrific assault by terrorists is not some expression of divine wrath. God did not do this, nor did God will it to happen. God has not "withdrawn" his protection because of our national sin, as though God normally shields our nation with some heavenly Star Wars program. This was an act of human terrorism and barbarity, not an act of divine judgment and retribution.

We who are followers of Jesus know that God was not in the hands of the hijackers, but in the torment of those who knew they were about to die. God was not looking down on the towers of the World Trade Center from a place of heavenly safety, but was suffering, struggling, and weeping in the rubble. God was not in the language of hate and fear that took control of the planes, but in the language of the love that some were able to communicate to their families through cell phones and e-mail messages.

Americans who follow the Christian faith now also know more about our common humanity. We understand better those in our world today who have suffered, and still suffer, the kind of terrorism we have suffered.

We are united in a new kind of grief. If, as Christians believe, God has revealed God's divine life to us in the vulnerability and suffering of Jesus, then God continues to be released in the vulnerability and suffering of every son and daughter of God today wherever they suffer, at the hands of whomsoever they suffer.

God does not speak the language of hatred and rejection in any circumstance, and we who claim the name of Christian cannot answer hatred with hatred. Nor shall we ever again be able to distance ourselves from the acts of terrorism that continue throughout the world.

As people of faith, we are grounded in the example of Jesus. An old Anglican priest, Father Keble Talbot, once said, so memorably, "At the worst time, Jesus did the best deed." In the midst of his own terror, pain, and abandonment, Jesus' actions and words were for others. On the eve of his own death, Jesus gave himself away to his friends, and even to his enemies, in a new and intimate way. And he gave us the example that, if we want to be like him, we too must do the best deeds at the worst times.

All people of faith know that religion can be perverted and used as a weapon of fear and hate. There are Christians who do that, Jews who do that, and Muslims who do that. We have been hearing such perversions of Christianity in our country, especially since the terrorist attacks. Christian fundamentalism of that sort is no different in its potential consequences from Jewish or Muslim fundamentalism.

People of faith also understand that those who use Christianity as a weapon do not define the Christian faith for the vast majority of Christians the world over. In a similar fashion, those who use the great faiths of Judaism and Islam to justify hate and violence do not define those great religious traditions, either.

Perhaps hardest of all, we who are grounded in faith know that, in the preacher Eric James's memorable words, "as deep as the cause of the patriot is in the American soul, the cause of the kingdom of God is greater even than that of the patriot." It is precisely our love of our country that must compel us to remember who we are as Christian people, and what both the ideals of our democracy and the requirements of our faith demand of us.

These are some of the chief groundings of faith that must guide us through the emotions of these tragic days. It is not an easy road, and the journey before us will take every ounce of moral and religious courage that we have.

But at our best, the people of God, Christians, Jews, and Muslims, are a living testimony to the faith that we can be called to a nobler life, a deeper communion, a more perfect way, and a new converted language.

The Rev. Canon Peter Eaton was rector at Saint James Episcopal Church, Lancaster, Pennsylvania, when this essay appeared in the Lancaster Sunday News *on September 30, 2001. He later became Dean of the Cathedral of Saint John in Denver, Colorado.*

Does God Make Everything Happen?

Cynthia Lapp

I am not overly attached to my children. I do not tear up at the first day of school or kiss them in their sleep. September 11 changed all of that.

School closed early that day. As I left the office to pick up my children, I determined to tell them the truth about the unfolding tragedy. They had been told nothing at school. I wanted to tell them privately about the unspeakable horrors of the morning.

When I picked up six-year-old Cecilia, her first comment was, "If God is in everyone, then God makes everything happen."

"It's true," I replied, "that God is in everyone, but sometimes people don't realize that and they do bad things. Today something terrible happened."

"Oh, I know," she said. "There was a big plane crash." Somehow she *had* heard. We talked about the tragedy and continued the conversation at home with her father, Eric.

As we sat down for dinner that evening, Cecilia prayed "for the people that were hurt in the plane crashes, and thank you, God, for telling us what happened." Three-year-old Jamie wondered if the planes were still crashing.

After dinner Jamie found a fire truck and ambulance that he had never played with before and showed Eric how they were helping at the attack site. As he prepared for sleep, Jamie lined up his ambulance, fire truck, and favorite stuffed animals as a barricade next to his bed. In the grocery store, two weeks later, Jamie wondered aloud, "Do the people here have guns?"

I continue the struggle to help my children live without fear even as I deal with my own. To help, I have begun singing a song, day and night, to alleviate our fear:

> Don't be afraid.
> My love is stronger;
> my love is stronger than your fear.
> Don't be afraid;
> my love is stronger.
> And I have promised to be always near. (John L. Bell)

My children and I are not the only ones living with fear. I remind myself, and sometimes Cecilia and Jamie, that children all over the world live without homes and with daily fear and hunger. Many children do not have parents or families to care for them.

All these years we have lived with a false sense of security. Our abundance of food and clothes as well as shelter, work, family, and friends can no longer be taken for granted. How do I teach my children that, while they are fortunate to have all these things, much of our wealth comes at the expense of others throughout the world?

Life has changed since September 11. Now I ask myself, "How will I change in response? How I will help my children understand in new ways that we are part of a larger world?"

At Jamie's initiative, we have begun to sing the "Continent Song" at dinner: "There are seven continents in the world. North America, South America, Europe, Asia,

Africa. Don't forget Australia, don't forget Antarctica. Seven continents in the world, tell me what they are."

It's small, but it's a start.

Cynthia Lapp formerly served with the Women's Alliance for Theology, Ethics and Ritual (WATER), Silver Spring, Maryland. Adapted from WATERwheel *(fall 2001), a quarterly newsletter. "Don't Be Afraid,"* © 1995, WGRG, Iona Community, Glasgow, Scotland.

How Can God Permit Suffering?

Frederica Mathewes-Green

When it hits home, we reel back. Thoughts explode in confusion: I trusted God, where is he? If he's all-powerful, why didn't he stop it? Maybe he doesn't love us. Maybe he is punishing us. Maybe he is weak. Are we really so alone and endangered? Can't we trust him? Are we so terrifyingly alone?

Suffering on this scale is new to us, but it is not new to the weary human race. Countless men and women before us have tried to understand God's presence in times of horror.

It's the big prize question of all spiritual life: how can bad things happen to good people? No matter how many words are poured over it, the problem remains, mocking us: good people still get clobbered by bad things. This, finally, is the problem. We don't want so much to know *why* it happens as to know *how to stop it* from happening, as if understanding what triggers such catastrophes might help us avoid them. Our quest is for prevention. Yet the cruel centuries keep rolling, and no one's yet found a way to prevent catastrophe.

The "problem of evil" and the alternatives have been cleverly summarized: "Either God is God and not good, or God is good and not God." That is, either God is not all loving in the way we think, and he tolerates our pain because his goals don't require our happiness. Or God suffers with us helplessly but is unable to stop our suffering and thus is not all-powerful. Neither alternative works.

A God who is not good would violate the definition and violate what we know of his overwhelming goodness running through most of our lives. A God who is not all-powerful would likewise void the meaning of the word. The retired Episcopal bishop of South Carolina, Fitzsimmons Allison, explained that accepting this confounding mystery is the only way to resolve it: "I've got the 'I don't know' theodicy. God is God, and God is good, and I don't know."

Through the ages, people have made many attempts to hammer out the dilemma. Maybe it is the devil wreaking his anger on the faithful. Maybe it is random effects from the initial fall of Adam and Eve, which sent a wave of disorder rolling obliviously forward through time. Maybe God won't stop bad people from hurting others, because then he'd have to stop everyone from doing even small bad things, and human history would become mere puppetry.

A world of free creatures requires the possibility that they may choose evil. Since the flood of Noah, God has declined to fix things by wiping out all the troublemakers. The only remaining solution is for each of us to realize that we ourselves are junior troublemakers to one extent or another, and that we must do our part to clean up our own corners.

This is why Jesus was always telling people to repent. He gave no other explanation of suffering. When an atrocity was reported to him—worshipers murdered in the temple itself—he rejected the idea that they suffered this because they were worse sinners than anyone else. Yet he concluded, "Unless you repent, you will all perish just as they did" (Luke 13:1-5). This is a hard word, one that doesn't often get preached on or written up in curly script on refrigerator magnets.

We keep asking "Why?" but we don't need to know why something happened. Moreover, we couldn't use that knowledge to go back in time and stop it. The terrifying truth is that we can't gather enough clues to know how to prevent it from happening next time. That's our real reason for so desperately asking why: we hope for enough clues to be able to protect ourselves from suffering again. But God does not give us such power. He reserves it to himself and challenges us to trust in him. At times like this, trust is very hard.

Theodicy nettles us, but the bottom line is that it's irrelevant. The only useful question in such a time is not "Why?" but "What next?" What should I do next? What should be my response to this ugly event? How can I bring the best out of it? How can God bring resurrection out of it?

That is, of course, what he did when his own Son was bleeding and crying out to him. He did not prevent the suffering and did not cut it short, but he completed it with resurrection. If this is true, it changes everything; if it is not true, Christians are pathetic fools, because it is on this that we have staked all our hopes. "If Christ has not been raised, your faith is futile and you are still in your sins. . . . If for this life only we have hoped in Christ, we are of all people most to be pitied" (1 Cor. 15:17, 19).

So, there you are. All we can do is persevere and trust that if Christ was raised, we who belong to Christ will also be raised, and all our suffering will be made right (1 Cor. 15:23). All we can do is cast ourselves more completely into the arms of God. Three times the psalmist repeats a cry of trust that we need for such an awful time: "Forsake me not, O LORD: O my God, be not far from me. Make haste to help me, O LORD my salvation" (Ps. 38:21-22, KJV).

Frederica Mathewes-Green is a writer, speaker, and pastor's wife in the Eastern Orthodox Church. Adapted from her book At the Corner of East and Now *(Jeremy P. Tarcher/Putnam).*

Who Speaks for God?

Christy J. Waltersdorff

In a time of crisis, who speaks for God?

In the weeks since the terrorist attacks of September 11, we have heard many voices claiming to speak for God. The terrorists claim that their holy war against the United States is in fact the will of God. Do they speak for God?

Television evangelists are claiming to speak for God as well. Indeed, Jerry Falwell claimed that God allowed the attacks and the deaths of thousands because of all of the so-called liberal groups with which he disagrees. Does he speak for God?

So who does speak for God? Do our politicians who gathered on the steps of the Capitol to sing "God bless America"? Does our president, who gave the order to begin bombing Afghanistan?

Does your pastor speak for God? Some think that is part of my job description. But my role as your pastor is to walk with you as, together, we interpret the Word of God, and together we experience the presence of Jesus Christ in our midst.

Who does speak for God? God speaks for God!

In the Old Testament, the people heard the word of God from the prophets. Often the real prophets were not popular because the people didn't always like what they had to say. But they said it anyway. Have we lost our ability to distinguish between true prophets and false prophets? Jeremiah was a true prophet of God, and he had the battle scars and the prison time to prove it.

Jeremiah thought the future lay with the exiles. They were the only ones who were ready and open for a future since they really had no present in which to trust. Everything they thought and believed had changed. But even then, before they could embrace a new future, they had to let go of the past and accept the present. They had to abandon the false hopes they placed in military rebellion and in trying to re-create what was already lost. They had to see their exile as the place where God would work most effectively.

Several months ago, when I decided to preach on this text from the lectionary (Jer. 29), I had no way of knowing how it would speak to us. I now believe, with the events of September 11, that we in the United States are in exile. And as people living in exile, we hear the words of the prophet Jeremiah in a new way. To be in exile is to be forcefully removed from one's country or home. I believe, in a sense, that is what happened on September 11.

An unimaginable act of violence forced us from the safety of the emotional country we considered our home. Exile is a time when all of the old certainties are gone, when everything we thought we were is gone, and everything we dreamed is gone. Sometimes forever.

Those living in exile need two things: they need to come to terms with the reality of where they are, and they need to have hope that there is a future. Exile brings with it anger and pain. It brings with it a sense of helplessness and, sometimes, hopelessness.

It also brings with it an opportunity for God to do something new. The voices of the Jeremiahs are the voices we need to be hearing right now.

God did not bring the terrorist attacks to make us better people. But I do believe that if we are open to God, God can work through this time of pain and sorrow. As Bob Gross reminds us, "Nothing that happened on September 11 changes anything about the Christian faith."

Maybe what has changed is our willingness to hear the call of God. As Christians, we live comfortably in the culture of the United States. In recent years, perhaps we haven't lifted our voices enough for the cause of peace.

Maybe this time of exile is the time we are to raise our voices and witness to the world in the name of the Prince of Peace, Jesus Christ. Maybe this time of exile is ripe for change. As followers of Christ, we have an opportunity to help shape that change.

Peace is not a message our nation wants to hear right now. As bombs pound Afghanistan further back into the Stone Age, the politicians and commentators speak of justice and the power of democracy. While innocent civilians are killed and others are forced out of their homes and into refugee camps, terrorists remain safe in their hideouts and recruit even more young men to their cause.

Wesley Granberg-Michaelson, general secretary of the Reformed Church in America, believes that our response to terrorism will test who we are. "In this 'campaign against terrorism,'" he says, "our strongest weapons are our ideals and values—our belief in the dignity and worth of every human life, our conviction that nations are strong only when they respect the rights of all, and our determination to pursue what is right in ways that are just."

This is why, he believes, our struggle is at heart a spiritual one. He believes that the church must insist on the distinction between justice and revenge. Our task is to resist being "overcome by evil," and instead to "overcome evil with good" (Rom. 12:21).

I doubt that there were many of us watching the twin towers collapse into a horrifying graveyard, who didn't want, at that moment, to see Osama bin Laden and his henchmen destroyed in a similar manner. But the church must plead with the nation never to forget who we say we are. Our gravest temptation at this hour is to be grasped by the same evil that controlled the terrorists. That is why we must pray fervently, "Lead us not into temptation, but deliver us from evil" (Matt. 6:13, KJV).

When we try to fight evil with evil, we will likely be overcome by it. We are overcome by evil not when something evil or violent happens to us, but when we use evil in response. And that is what we must guard against in these days. It is too easy—in the fever pitch of patriotism and "America right or wrong" thinking—to get sucked into "an eye for an eye" mode of thinking and acting (Exod. 21:24).

Gandhi reminded us that "an eye for an eye just makes everybody blind."

I call us today to seek a new path, a different path. A path of justice grounded in our faith in Jesus Christ, grounded in our hope in a faithful God. Our hope in God finds reassurance in Psalm 66. In this psalm the community of faith recalls its time of difficulty, when other people rode over their heads, when they went through fire and water. It was a terrible time, but they were never outside the care and concern of God. The people do not see this time as rejection by God or punishment from God. Their focus is on the release and restoration by God.

The prophet Jeremiah reminds us that God wants good things for the exiles. God wants good things for all people. Jeremiah tells us, "For surely I know the plans I have for you, says the Lord, plans for your welfare and not for harm, to give you a future with hope" (Jer. 29:11).

In this time of grief, pain, anger, uncertainty, and rage, we are called to be faithful to the God we know through Jesus Christ.

My prayer of hope is that one day the people of the earth will proclaim the words from the psalm, "Come and see what God has done!" (Ps. 66:5). And they will know that, through our time of exile, we were instruments of peace in bringing God's shalom into reality.

May it be so. Amen.

Christy J. Waltersdorff pastors the York Center Church of the Brethren, Lombard, Illinois. Adapted from a sermon, October 14, 2001.

Chapter 2

Jesus and the Way of Peace

The events of September 11 have raised a host of religious questions. Retail stores reported soaring sales of books on Islam, faith, and suffering. Newspapers and magazines overflowed with stories about Islam as many Americans, for the first time, scrambled to understand Islam and their Muslim neighbors.

For many centuries the Christian tradition has wrestled with the question of violence. The life of Jesus and the practice of the early church embodied nonviolent responses to evil and sought to overcome evil with good. Yet history shows us that the Christian church has also engaged in violent crusades against Muslims and supported "just" wars as well as traditional pacifism.

For Christians, Jesus is understood as God's full and definitive revelation. Yet few popular writers or journalists have explored the life and teachings of Jesus in the context of September 11. In chapter 2, a variety of writers examine Jesus' way of peace as they search for guidance and direction in the valley of the shadow of fear.

What Would Jesus Do?

Donald B. Kraybill

For many Americans, the events of September 11 provoked a flurry of questions about Islam. What did Muhammad really say about jihad? Is Islam a peace-loving religion? Does the Koran justify killing? Were the terrorists Islamic extremists or mainstream Muslims? These pressing questions quickly spiked sales of the Koran and stirred scholarly debate. Indeed, the answers to these questions will likely shape international perceptions for years to come.

Curiously, however, few were asking about Jesus. Surely what Jesus had to say might shape international events as well. In recent years the well-worn words "What Would Jesus Do?" or "WWJD?" have appeared on bracelets and all sorts of trinkets promoting the Christian faith. Why, however, were so few people asking "WWJD?" after September 11?

Perhaps the answer was already clear. Perhaps we assumed that all the renditions of "God Bless America" reflected the sentiments of Jesus. Or perhaps Jesus was simply forgotten in the scramble to decipher Muhammad.

There may be another reason for the silence. Perhaps we don't want to hear what Jesus has to say: "Love your enemies. Do not resist an evildoer. Pray for those who persecute you" (cf. Matt. 5:44, 39, 11). On the cross, suffering a cruel death, Jesus pleads, "Father, forgive them; for they do not know what they are doing" (Luke 23:34). This is the prophet who called his followers to forgive seventy times seven (Matt.

18:22, KJV). Forgiveness lies at the heart of the Lord's Prayer. Jesus calls his disciples to love their enemies, to be like God, who shines the sun on the evil and the good, and showers rain on the just and the unjust (Matt. 5:45).

The teachings of Jesus are clear. He taught forgiveness and love for the enemy, and explicitly rejected revenge and retaliation. "You have heard that it was said, 'You shall love your neighbor and hate your enemy.' But I say to you, Love your enemies" (Matt. 5:43-44). Beyond mere words, Jesus lived nonviolence even as it led to his agonizing death on a cross. In the face of terror and abuse, he did not retaliate or even defend himself. As God's highest and final revelation, Jesus disclosed an uncommon kind of God.

This God doesn't fight. Most gods relish conquest and military victory. This God is willing to suffer and die. This God contends that evil can be overcome by good. This is not a god of chariots and swords, but a God of stables and donkeys, who willingly suffers and dies on a cross. Suffering and forgiveness are his answer to evil. As Gordon Houser notes, "Jesus, not soldiers, set us free. He died for our sins; he did not kill for them."

Perhaps this is why so few people were asking about Jesus after September 11. In the midst of our rage, we didn't want to hear these words, let alone practice them. The embrace of the enemy and the willingness of Jesus to die on a cross are scandalous. This outrageous vulnerability is the most distinctive feature of the Christian faith. Unlike other gods, this one doesn't fight. This God is willing to suffer and die for the sake of righteousness.

The unmistakable teachings of Jesus have troubled Christians over the centuries. They challenge our natural impulses for defense, protection, and revenge. His nonviolent teachings silence our urge for revenge. They offer a nonviolent way of cutting the bloody, spiraling cycle of violence. As Jesus said, it is one thing to love those who love us back, but an entirely different thing to love our enemies, especially when they are terrorists (Matt. 5:46).

Jesus' teachings raise two basic questions: (1) May the followers of Jesus use lethal force for personal self-defense? (2) May they use violent means to protect a neighbor? We can address these questions on *two* levels: personal behavior and societal behavior.

Over the centuries, the nonviolent teachings of Jesus have created problems for those who bear his name. Thus, many Christians have constructed detours around his message of nonviolence. Consider some of the detours.

Some have argued that because the Hebrew Scriptures support warfare, we should turn to them for guidance during times of war. Plenty of verses in the Hebrew Bible can be used to support taking part in war. But this detour creates problems for Christians who see Jesus as God's fullest and final revelation. Jesus himself was emphatic: "You have heard that it *was* said, ... But I say to you, Love your enemies."

Other Christians contend that Jesus only came to die as our Savior. Thus, his death is all that matters, and what he said or did doesn't matter much as long as people accept him as Savior. In other words, "WWJD?" doesn't matter. This spiritualized version of Jesus renders his life and nonviolent teachings irrelevant for daily living.

Somewhat akin to this is the view that when Jesus was talking about loving enemies, he was referring to pie in the sky by and by, about how things would be in paradise when his kingdom came in its fullness.

Others have said that Jesus was simply talking about personal ethics and behavior, not about social ethics and national policy. So we should try to love our personal enemies and not retaliate when we face injustice. With this view, enemy love is not applicable to political or national enemies. Jesus, they claim, offers guidance for personal behavior but not for group behavior.

All of these detours render Jesus irrelevant for the pressing issues prompted by September 11; yet everyone wants to know about Muhammad. Jesus is understood, but few want to listen, or more precisely, few are willing to follow him. Who wants to die on a cross or practice love of enemies when it flies in the face of basic common sense? Yet many are willing to die in combat.

For those who name Jesus as Lord and affirm that he is God's fullest and final revelation, things are different. His teachings of love, mercy, and forgiveness are admonitions for faithful disciples, not just sweet utopian dreams.

Nevertheless, the vexing question for those who name the name of Jesus and seek to follow in his way is this: Can we kill someone under any circumstances?

As the events of September 11 have shown, evil and violence are real. Revenge and retaliation fill the air. How do disciples of Jesus demonstrate the love of God without using violent means? How do they respond without becoming the very evil they deplore? How do we overcome evil with good?

As a disciple of Jesus, I cannot kill or use violent means. I could use nonlethal force to restrain evildoers, but I could not in good conscience participate in violence that takes the life of another person. If I were faced with a situation where, by taking a life, I could prevent enormous destruction to other lives, I would certainly be tempted to use violence. But if I did take a life under such circumstances, I would see it as sin and would need to beg for forgiveness.

It is clear what Jesus would *not* do when faced with terrorist attacks. The evidence from his life shows that he rejected violence and retaliation. All this makes things uncomfortable for those who bear his name because we too are pulled toward rage and revenge. We want safety and protection and an end to fear and terrorist threats. We want the perpetrators of these dastardly deeds held accountable. While it mocks common sense and popular opinion, I have no choice but to seek nonviolent ways of overcoming evil if I want to bear the name of Jesus with integrity.

Donald B. Kraybill *is Professor of Sociology and Anabaptist Studies at Messiah College, Grantham, Pennsylvania.*

How Strong Is Love?

Linda Gehman Peachey

The Sermon on the Mount has long been a guide for those who seek to follow Jesus' example and teachings. Here Jesus gives specific instructions to his disciples, including how to respond when mistreated. Especially after a horrific attack such as on September 11, these teachings may appear divorced from reality and hopelessly naive, even dangerous. How can Jesus counsel us to "turn the other cheek"? Can he mean for us to be so passive in the face of evil?

We often read these teachings with little understanding of Jesus' social setting. We tend to see Jesus passively accepting mistreatment from opponents but do not see that he was engaged in a campaign to include those who had been excluded or ostracized.

The Gospel of Matthew highlights the conflict between Jesus and other religious leaders over the question of obedience to the law and the prophets. They clash over keeping the Sabbath, observing purity laws, and worshiping in the temple. We usually understand these as conflicts over religious issues. In fact, they often reflected profound social and economic issues of that time.

Jesus did not oppose these laws in principle; what he rejected was the way in which these laws excluded people. Strict observance of the Sabbath and purity laws, for example, left out a large part of the people living in Palestine. The same was true of the requirement for temple sacrifice in order to receive forgiveness. It was not that people refused to worship God but that they were often so destitute that they simply could not keep these laws. Or they were automatically excluded because of illness and disability or because they were women, Samaritans, or Gentiles.

Jesus' healing and teaching ministry was thus a "civil rights" campaign to include the poor, outcasts, and outsiders. They too were children of God and deserving of dignity. They too could worship God and receive God's love and blessing. And God would grant forgiveness even without temple sacrifice, simply if one was willing to forgive others.

In this context, the Sermon on the Mount takes on a new dimension. Jesus' teachings on anger, for instance, no doubt grew out of deep concern that he and his followers not jeopardize their message of love and inclusion by overreacting in harmful ways. As they faced opposition, any angry or insulting response to their challengers could have led to charges before a judge or council. They also had to maintain harmony among themselves and not give any opening for their antagonists to discredit them. Since they were seeking respect and inclusion for all, they needed to model those values. Their actions and attitudes had to be above reproach.

Similar issues underlie Jesus' instructions about retaliation. We often read these as demanding meek submission to evil. Yet I believe that in Jesus' time and setting, they were a call to creative, nonviolent resistance. For example, the Greek word here for "resist" was often used as a military term. A better translation is "Do not resist an evildoer with violence" (Matt. 5:39). This fits the command elsewhere in the New Testament: "Do not repay anyone evil for evil" (Rom. 12:17-21; 1 Thess. 5:15; 1 Peter 3:9).

Jesus provides several examples of creative responses to wrong. Being struck on the right cheek was not about a fistfight between equals (Matt. 5:39). Instead, this was likely a backhanded, insulting slap in the face from a "superior." A servant who responded by turning the other cheek was making an assertive response, redefining the situation and asking a contemptuous master to recognize one's humanity: "If you are going to strike me, do so as equal."

Being sued for one's cloak, as a guarantee for a loan, also speaks to oppression (Matt. 5:40). Hebrew law gives specific guidance about such transactions and forbids creditors from keeping a debtor's cloak overnight since he may need it for warmth (Exod. 22:25-27). A destitute person who follows Jesus' counsel and hands over both inner and outer garments, unmasks the injustice of a legal system that allows people to be robbed of all they have. Exposing oneself in such a way would expose the naked intent of one's masters.

Roman soldiers could compel civilians to carry their

heavy packs for a stretch. Under a military occupation, such a duty was deeply hated and carried out with sullen and bitter resentment. Volunteering to go a second mile would certainly surprise the soldier and throw him into anxious confusion (Matt. 5:41). What does this person want? What is his intention? Again, such an action allows the weaker party to seize the initiative and force the stronger party to recognize that he does not have complete control.

No doubt Jesus recognized that it would be utterly futile for the Jewish people to fight Roman occupation on their terms. As noted by James Douglass *(The Nonviolent Coming of God)*, Jesus came to live in Nazareth just a few years after Roman armies had destroyed Sepphoris, a large city just four miles to the north. Growing up, he likely heard stories about the uprising that led to this catastrophe, about the fires that raged and the crucifixion of 2,000 people, carried out as a dire warning against any further revolts. Clearly, there had to be another way to peace and justice for his people.

Like the prophets before him, Jesus urged his people to act justly toward one another, and to see that God's love extends even to their enemies. Indeed, Jesus claimed that love has tremendous power and is ultimately stronger than even the greatest weapons.

Gandhi called this love "satyagraha," the force born of truth and love. Far from passive submission to evil, this force uses the power of love to resist personal, social, economic, and political exploitation. Indeed, Gandhi believed that this love is more powerful than military force because it allows one to know and experience God. He told his followers that if their embrace of nonviolence made them feel weaker rather than stronger, it would be better for them to take up arms. Nonviolence is not for the weak but for those who are strong

(Eknath Easwaran, *A Man to Match His Mountains*).

What might Jesus tell us after September 11? How might we resist the evil of terrorism in a loving, nonviolent way? Certainly, we are still searching for answers. We will need to fast and pray, listen and think, brainstorm and experiment.

We can begin by stressing our common humanity. Violence and oppression occur most often where people are seen as less than human or demonized. The power of Jesus' examples is in showing how people can seize the initiative and surprise the other into seeing the situation in a new way.

What response would most surprise and challenge those who support terrorism against us? What would best help them to see us as good and compassionate people?

What if we embarked on a serious effort to help Afghanistan rebuild after so many years of drought and war? What if we helped to address the serious economic and political problems that feed despair and frustration in the Middle East? Indeed, our government does recognize the need to address some of these humanitarian needs. Yet, to be effective, what is needed is the equivalent of the Marshall Plan that helped rebuild Germany after World War II.

This does not mean that those who planned these attacks should go free. As with all who commit criminal acts, they should be found and held accountable. They should have to face what they have done and be prosecuted according to international laws.

Still, the road to peace and security will be long and difficult. As we search for solutions, Jesus invites us to actively use the strength of this love that is indeed more powerful than hate and stronger than terror.

Linda Gehman Peachey is a freelance writer of Lancaster, Pennsylvania.

Loving the Terrorists

David Diggs

I consider myself a Christian, at least some of the time. Other times, if I'm honest with myself, I'm not much of a Christian at all. Following Christ just seems too hard. What happened on September 11 has made it feel almost impossible to follow Jesus.

Many early followers of Jesus found it possible to love and forgive their enemies even while they or their loved ones were being fed to the lions. I read of Stephen, whose last words while being stoned to death by religious zealots were, "Lord, do not hold this sin against them" (Acts 7:60).

Among those at Stephen's stoning was a young religious extremist named Saul (Acts 8:1-3). One day while in fanatical pursuit of heretics, he had a blinding encounter with the resurrected Jesus (Acts 9). The experience turned his world upside down. Saul became the apostle Paul and one of history's greatest advocates of Jesus. As miraculous as the conversion of this terrorist was, it was even more remarkable that the people he had ruthlessly terrorized forgave him and took him in as one of their own (9:26-27).

With Saul's conversion, this hunter became the prey. Like those he had once terrorized, he became a victim, paying for his devotion to Christ with regular imprisonments and torture. Like Stephen, he died a martyr. Not long before his arrest at Jerusalem, he wrote from Corinth to encourage fellow Christians facing stiff persecution in Rome:

Bless those who persecute you; bless and do not curse. . . . Do not repay anyone evil for evil. Be careful to do what is right in the eyes of everybody. If it is possible, as far as it depends on you, live at peace with everyone. Do not take revenge, my friends, but leave room for God's wrath, for it is written: "It is mine to avenge; I will repay," says the Lord. On the contrary: "If your enemies are hungry, feed them; if they are thirsty, give them something to drink. In doing this, you will heap burning coals on their head." Do not be overcome by evil, but overcome evil with good. (Rom. 12:15, 17-21, NIV, with "enemy" pluralized)

Paul's words were not ignored. The lives of the Christian martyrs show a love that seems as fanatical and extreme as the hatred we witnessed on September 11.

Where in their hearts did these followers of Jesus find such love for those who hunted them down so ruthlessly? I can only understand their love as an outpouring of the love they found in Christ. At the heart of their faith was their assurance of Christ loving humanity so much that to make peace with us he submitted to the cruelest torture and humiliation of the time. By loving their enemies and returning good for evil, they served as vessels of this same radical, redeeming love they saw displayed on the cross of Christ.

How tragic that within a few hundred years the cross became, for the world, *not* the symbol of the infinite love of God, but the standard raised before crusaders marching and murdering to rid the world of the "infidel" Muslims and Jews who "polluted" the Holy Land. Even today, for millions of Muslims and Jews, the cross says nothing of love. Instead, it is a symbol of bigotry, hatred, and aggression, like the burning crosses of the KKK.

Today many are quick to point out that this jihad the terrorists have declared has nothing to do with the true teachings of Islam, and that Islam is peace-loving. I'm grateful for this reminder. I just hope someone tells Muslims around the world that the bombs the USA drops on their brothers and sisters, have nothing to do with the true teachings of Christ. Bombing our enemies might satisfy our thirst for vengeance. But killing people who have already shown an unflinching willingness to die for their cause will only make more martyrs, and will give a whole new generation more to fight and die for.

Martin Luther King Jr. speaks to us today with his warning, "If you succumb to the temptation of using violence in the struggle, unborn generations will be the recipients of a long and desolate night of bitterness, and your chief legacy will be an endless reign of meaningless chaos."

As Judy Keane said after her husband, Richard, was killed in the attack, "The World Trade Center [attack] was in retaliation for something else, and that was the retaliation for something else. Are we going to continue this in perpetuity? We have to say at some point, 'Okay, let's find another way of doing this.'" Jesus points us to other ways.

There is no guarantee that our love will soften terrorists' hearts and end their attacks. Just look at what happened to Paul, Stephen, and Christ. The decision to love our enemies should not be made because it is more likely to bring success, but because it is the only way to be faithful to Christ.

In the same sermon where Jesus calls us to love our enemies, he tells us, "Blessed are those who mourn" (Matt. 5:4). Later he weeps with the family of dead Lazarus (John 11:35). In the spirit of Jesus, Paul says, "Weep with those who weep" (Rom. 12:15). I believe Jesus is mourning with us who have suffered from these attacks. Just as he wept over Jerusalem, he weeps over New York and Washington and our whole nation (Matt. 23:37-39).

While Jesus mourns with us, though, he also mourns with those who consider us their enemy. He mourns with the Palestinian mother whose husband and children were killed by a U.S.-supplied rocket, and with the Afghan father whose baby died from malnutrition. He mourns not only our loss of 7,000 people in the attacks of September 11, but also the deaths of roughly 24,000 people around our globe who died from hunger on September 11. Their deaths were not so visible as those at the World Trade Center, but Jesus sees them and mourns with those who loved them no less than he mourns with us.

If we were more like Jesus and able to mourn with those who mourn around the globe, I believe we would lose our taste for war and vengeance. We would no longer be able to waste our money on things we don't really need. We wouldn't let our government spend nearly a billion dollars a day on guns, bombs, and soldiers, while over a billion people worldwide struggle to survive on less than a dollar a day.

We would know that, as our former president General Dwight Eisenhower said, "Every gun that is made, every warship launched, every rocket fired, signifies in the final sense a theft from those who hunger and are not fed, those who are cold and are not clothed."

Let us vow to waste no more energy on violence and no more money on arms. As World Vision founder Bob Pierce used to say, "Let us allow our hearts to be broken by the things that break the heart of God," whether from terrorism in the USA or hunger in Afghanistan or Haiti or anywhere.

Following Jesus is rarely easy. We've been wounded; it is natural to want to fight back. My prayer is that, in this time of pain and mourning, we will open ourselves up and allow the limitless love of Christ to flow through us to our enemies. In doing so, we will be opening our wounded hearts to the healing that only God's love can bring. The love we have for our enemies will be a balm to our own hurts.

May God strengthen all of us who seek to follow Christ, to put aside our vain trust in swords, guns, and bombs. May we, instead, put our faith in the One who loves us and our enemies beyond comprehension.

May the fanatical and extreme love displayed on the cross overflow in us, comfort us, and free us to love all whom Jesus loves—even our enemies, the terrorists.

David Diggs serves on staff with Beyond Borders. Adapted from an essay at www.BeyondBorders.net.

Jesus and Muhammad
Two Roads to Peace

David W. Shenk

"Jesus the Messiah was not crucified; he escaped the cross!" insisted the Muslim theologian Shabir Ali in a Coventry University dialogue with me a year ago.

For six intense days in October 2000, Shabir Ali and I dialogued on the gospel and Islam with university audiences in the United Kingdom. The crucifixion of the Messiah drew the most intense differences. Islam denies that Jesus the Messiah was crucified. Christians confess that his crucifixion and resurrection are central events in history. Shabir Ali and I knew that the theological significance of our disagreement was profound. It is the core difference between Koranic (Qur'anic) and New Testament understandings of peace.

These different understandings of peace are revealed in two journeys: Jesus from Galilee to Jerusalem, and Muhammad from Mecca to Medina.

Jesus' Journey. In Galilee Jesus miraculously fed some five thousand people through the breaking of five loaves of bread and two fish. Immediately, Galilean leaders eagerly invited Jesus to become their king (John 6:1-15). Zealot freedom fighters were nearby in the Galilean hills. They could have been recruited for the army of King Jesus. He could feed the troops miraculously. They would fight the Romans and establish the rule of God throughout the earth, just as the prophets had promised the Messiah would do.

Jesus rejected the invitation to become their king. Instead, "he set his face to go to Jerusalem" (Luke 9:51). He did not hurry the journey. He taught and healed along the way. But he told his disciples that the journey to Jerusalem would end in crucifixion (Matt. 16:21). They could not believe it. The disciples accepted that Jesus was indeed "the Messiah, the Son of the living God" (16:16), but they "knew" that the Messiah could not be crucified!

Peter even rebuked Jesus for thinking about crucifixion. Jesus' response was sharp: "Get behind me, Satan! You are a stumbling block to me; for you are setting your mind not on divine things but on human things" (Matt. 16:23).

As Jesus entered Jerusalem, he rode on a colt (Luke 19:29-45). Centuries earlier Zechariah had prophesied that the King who rides into Jerusalem on a colt will "proclaim peace to the nations. His rule will extend from sea to sea and from the

River to the ends of the earth" (Zech. 9:9-10, NIV). By riding on the colt, Jesus announced that he was the King. The children were jubilant, but the authorities were furious.

When Jesus and the army of singing children came to the Mount of Olives, he wept, because Jerusalem would not receive the things that made for peace (Luke 19:41-42). Then Jesus and the children entered the temple. He chased the merchants from the temple as the children sang. In cleansing the temple, Jesus proclaimed a peace embracing justice: his "house" would be for "all the nations" (Mark 11:17).

Events moved quickly. At the private Passover meal, Jesus revealed to the disciples that Judas would betray him (Mark 14:18). Then in an act of astonishing service, Jesus arose from the table and washed the feet of each disciple (John 13). The seating arrangement suggests that Jesus first washed the feet of Judas. He even gave Judas a piece of bread dipped in broth from his own dish (Mark 14:20). Yet Judas rejected these invitations. Later that night he betrayed Jesus (14:43).

During his arrest, Jesus rebuked Peter for using a sword in his defense (John 18:11). He explained that earthly kingdoms use the sword, but not the kingdom of God that he was inaugurating (18:36). At his trial Jesus said he could call legions of angels to his defense, but he would not (Matt. 26:52-53). He was beaten and reviled. His disciples forsook him. He was crucified between two thieves. His outstretched wounded arms and hands on that cross revealed God's love and vulnerability. He cried out, "Father forgive them; for they do not know what they are doing" (Luke 23:34).

Oswald Chambers has commented that the crucifixion shows "our sins crashing into God." Those open wounded hands are "God with Us," the God we have pierced. These open arms and hands invite us into his forgiving and reconciling embrace. In that forgiveness and reconciliation, there is peace, with God and with one another. The faithful church gathers in the name of Jesus crucified and risen. The church is the fellowship of forgiveness and peace, a new people re-created through the Spirit of Jesus to be a people of peace, who forgive, love, serve, and suffer as Jesus did.

The witness of the New Testament church is that this "Christ crucified" is "the power of God" (1 Cor. 1:23-24).

Muhammad's Journey. Six centuries later, Muhammad proclaimed Islam, the submission to God that is peace. However, Muhammad chose a different path from Jesus in seeking the peace that Islam offers. Islamic teaching says the angel Gabriel revealed the Koran (Qur'an) to Muhammad. For twelve years after the revelations began, Muhammad preached in his hometown of Mecca. He was ridiculed, and his disciples were persecuted. Muhammad and his followers faced a major theological dilemma: If Muhammad is a prophet of God, why do he and his followers suffer?

The theological crisis was profound. Then a delegation from Medina invited Muhammad to come to their city and become their prophet and also their statesman. Muhammad accepted the invitation, and he and his followers began the secret pilgrimage from Mecca to Medina.

This pilgrimage, the Hijrah, is the beginning of the Muslim era. That era does not start with the prophet's birth or the revelations that came to him, but with the Hijrah. Why is this so important theologically? The Hijrah shows that Muhammad is indeed a prophet of God, for in Medina he had the power to establish the Muslim community *(ummah)*.

The Koran says, "And when those who disbelieve plot against thee (O Muhammad) to wound thee fatally, or to kill thee or to drive thee forth; they plot, but Allah also plotteth;

and Allah is the best of plotters" (Anfal [8]:30).

As long as Muhammad was a suffering prophet in Mecca, he could not establish the Muslim ummah; individuals could submit to the peace of Islam, but a community of peace did not emerge. However, in Medina he was prophet, statesman, and military commander. With these combined powers, he could defend and establish the peace of Islam, not only for individuals, but for an entire city and eventually all of Arabia.

The Muslims used this political-military power skillfully. In Medina, the Muslim ummah established the *dar al salaam* (region of peace). This is the area governed by the Muslims. The Medinan Muslims viewed the world as divided into two regions. There is peace in the dar al salaam. However, the *dar al harb* (region of war) is not yet ruled by Muslims and is therefore outside the rule of peace.

A duty of the dar al salaam is to protect the rights of groups such as Christians. The Koran reminds Muslim leaders that "there is no compulsion in religion" (Baqara [2]:256). Muslims invite other people to believe, but the choice to become a Muslim must be voluntary. However, when Islam or the community of faith is under threat, the Koran commands, "Fight in the way of Allah against those who fight against you. And fight them until persecution is no more, and religion is for Allah" (Baqara [2]:90-192).

The Muslim community has a mission to extend the region of peace until all people have the blessing of being ruled by Muslim political authority. Only Muslim political authority can transform culture and society in accord with the will of God. Muslims living in regions not under Muslim rule have incomplete peace. Only within the dar al salaam is peace fully established. Political power and peace belong together, as do personal piety and community peace.

Within Muhammad's lifetime, the peace of Islam was established throughout Arabia. Eight years after the Hijrah, Muhammad entered Mecca, leading ten thousand soldiers. The Meccan opposition had been defeated in earlier battles with the Muslims. At this time the city accepted the rule of the dar al salaam without resistance, and Muhammad declared, "Truth had come and falsehood hath vanished away!" (Bani Israil [17]:81).

According to Islamic theology, the sovereign, powerful Creator does not suffer. He is invulnerable and defends truth forcefully if necessary. This is why Muslims deny the crucifixion of Jesus. They believe Jesus is the Messiah, though in the Koran the meaning of *Messiah* is a mystery. Yet Muslims insist that the Messiah could never be crucified if he was a blessed prophet of God. Within Islamic theology, a crucified Messiah is impossible. Speaking of the Messiah, the Koran says, "But they killed him not, nor crucified him, but so he was made to appear to them" (Nisaa [4]: 157).

Surprised by Suffering. Both Christianity and Islam invite people into peace. However, the peace offered by the crucified Messiah is quite different from the peace of Islam. Muslim theologians frequently remind me, "There is nothing surprising in Islam, for Islam is natural." Indeed, the choice of Muhammad to become both a prophet and a statesman is fully understandable. This is the way nations and religions normally seek the peace. Yet in Jesus crucified, God turns our expectations upside down. One cannot overstate the astounding surprise that the kingdom of God breaks into history in the Messiah crucified—and risen. There is nothing "natural" about this. This is the amazement of the gospel.

Nevertheless, many Christians also deny the peace offered through the cross. The church has often combined political power, military might, conquest, and the gospel. The conflict flowing from September 11 reminds Muslims of the legacy of the Christian crusading wars against the dar al salaam.

There is a struggle going on between a peace established by military and political power on one hand, and on the other hand the peace revealed in the vulnerable crucified Messiah. This struggle lives within our own souls and is not just a struggle between two faith systems. We often turn away from the peace of the Messiah, who became a servant, "humbled himself and became obedient to death—even death on a cross" (Phil. 2:8, NIV). However, whenever the church embraces the peace offered by Christ, it becomes a reconciling and peacemaking fellowship.

Several conversations show this reality. Two acquaintances of mine met with King Hussein of Jordan (now dead). He said he appreciated the forgiving and reconciling spirit he often observed within the church. The king noted that he personally gave his family and government five thousand copies of a book written by a Palestinian Christian bishop, Abuna Shakur, describing the reconciling way of the Messiah. The king then surprised his guests by saying, "In the Middle East, the church is the only hope for reconciliation."

Several years ago three Muslim friends stayed in our home overnight. During breakfast the senior among them asked, "Why are Christians so engaged in peacemaking?"

We replied, "Peace is the gift of the Messiah, who suffered and was crucified. As he died, he proclaimed forgiveness for all who crucify him."

"That is impossible, for the Messiah was anointed with the power of God, and Power cannot suffer."

"Let God be God," we pled. "Do not say that God cannot express suffering love for his enemies!"

In October 2001, I met with Central Asian pastors for a seminar that compared the journeys to peace modeled by Jesus and Muhammad. It was a day touched with pathos, for all these pastors were leading congregations that were minority communities among Muslims. They hoped and prayed that the witness of the gospel would not be compromised in the Afghanistan conflict.

"Do American Christians and churches support the way of Christ?" asked a pastor.

There is nothing surprising about the American government's response to the September calamity. As I read it, most of the world does not believe it is a wise response, but it is not a surprising response. This is the way nations act, even though such confrontations and violence usually only intensify hatred. It is sad that the way of Christ is used to bless such national behavior, especially military action.

What about the church? These Central Asian pastors longed for a different message from their North American partner churches. At a time like this, a clear witness and commitment to the way of the cross is an astounding surprise. It would be good news indeed. If North American Christians believe that Jesus Christ is Lord, then this is a most critical time in the life of the global church. It is a time for North American Christians to clearly proclaim through action and witness that Christ crucified is the power of God. That kind of witness can surprise the whole world and also be a healing witness around the world.

David W. Shenk is former dean of Lithuania Christian College. Adapted from an article in the German Anabaptist-Mennonite magazine Die Brücke (The bridge), *no. 6, 2001 (www.mennoniten.de/diebruecke).*

Is Jesus Lord?

Darrin W. Belousek

As my initial shock passed on September 11, I felt moral outrage and also an intense desire to see the terrorists squashed. Recognizing this violence lurking in my own soul makes Jesus' call to nonviolence so compelling. Yet this is not just a matter of personal conviction. I am convinced that every Christian must face this question: Is Jesus Lord, or not?

The apostolic witness is that Jesus is Lord and Sovereign, the single power and authority to whom alone we owe ultimate loyalty and allegiance (Matt. 28:18; Acts 2:36; Phil. 2:9-11). The demands of nation are relativized by Jesus' command that our love be perfect, extending even to our enemies (Matt. 5:43-48). This implies that the claims of nation-state—including the call for us to kill our world neighbors and destroy their homes, whether in the name of "freedom," "justice," or "country," or anything else—are trumped by the claims of Jesus: "We must obey God rather than any human authority" (Acts 5:29).

If Jesus is Lord and Sovereign, then without exception or excuse, the law of perfect love must rule in our hearts and minds, in our words and deeds. The Christian must in *all* things deny oneself of vengeance, retaliation, and retribution, and abstain from violence and bloodshed. If, on the other hand, it is permissible for the Christian to commit violence, then Jesus cannot be Lord. Instead, another authority commands our loyalty and allegiance.

When Jesus asks for my life—"Those who find their life will lose it, and those who lose their life for my sake will find it" (Matt. 10:39)—he asks for my words and deeds as well as my thoughts and feelings. When the government calls me to fight, it also demands my life. It not only wants me to kill with my hands, but to do so out of love for country and hatred for a dehumanized enemy. It asks me to lose my life for the sake of the nation.

These are competing and irreconcilable demands, to follow Jesus' call to love my enemy, *and* to obey the nation's call to kill the enemy. Trying to do both requires me to separate myself into two persons, an inner person who thinks and feels, and an outer person who speaks and acts. This inner person, subject to the lordship of Christ, loves the enemy in mind and heart; the outer person is subject to the nation, answers its command, and kills the enemy.

But I cannot detach my thoughts and feelings from my words and deeds; to do so would compromise my basic integrity as a whole person. I am not only a mind that thinks and a heart that feels, but also a body that speaks and acts. My life as a person created in the image of God is all these things taken together. Thus, if I permit the nation to control me so that I am dutifully bound to kill the same enemy that Jesus commands me to love, this forces me either to deny that Christ is Lord or to live in fraud.

As in every war, there is much loose talk that pacifism is cowardly, irresponsible, and traitorous. If you're not for killing the terrorists, you cast your lot with them and against us and, hence, are for killing us. This false dichotomy—kill the enemy or join him—is seductive even for Christians.

Jesus proclaims, "Love your enemies" (Matt. 5:44). He said this while the most powerful and violent empire of his day occupied his country and routinely murdered thousands of his fellows. He did not teach his followers to respond to violence with violence, by which one only imitates the evil one hates. Instead, Jesus taught us to respond with blessing (Luke 6:28; cf. Rom. 12:14; 1 Cor. 4:12). This strategy led to his death by the same enemies he told his friends to love.

How might we respond to the events of September 11 with blessing rather than violence? We could feed the people of Afghanistan and Iraq and rebuild their infrastructure, destroyed by decades of war and sanctions. We could rebuild Palestinian homes and replant ancient olive groves illegally bulldozed by Israeli troops. We could—at a cost less than a sustained barrage of "smart" bombs and cruise missiles—create a new Marshall Plan for the Middle East and South Central Asia. Instead of "draining the swamp," as our government proposes, we could create oases of human communities flourishing in the desert.

Which, I ask, is more likely to reduce hate and resentment toward the United States? Which is more likely to quell the rising tide of religious and political violence, and to win the friendship of the peoples of the Middle East and South Central Asia? Bombing their countries, destroying their homes, and killing their women and children? Or feeding their hungry, housing their homeless, and healing their sick?

Why not do these acts of blessing instead of waging war? You laugh and say, "It won't work." But have we ever seriously considered, much less tried, such a thing? "Military intelligence" repeats its mantra that we must destroy the village to save it. But have we ever really tried to save our enemy's village *before* destroying it?

Darrin W. Belousek *teaches philosophy at Goshen (Ind.) College.*

Christ's Way of Peace

The Church of the Brethren

We challenge ourselves to a sacrificial commitment to Christ's way of peace. Creating a world of peace and security for all is a monumental task—one that can only be undertaken through the empowerment of God's Spirit and with the extraordinary commitment of God's people. We call on our congregations and members: To recommit themselves to seeking peace in their daily lives and relationships. To reaffirm the historic Church of the Brethren objection to war. To prayerfully consider their loyalties to their nation in light of their prior loyalty to God. To work for justice in the global community. And to creatively and nonviolently challenge the prevailing belief that the application of force is the path to enduring peace.

We believe that peace and security will not be found through military, economic, and political reprisal, or in the drastic curtailment of civil liberties in the United States. These avenues may satisfy the desire for retaliation and the appearance of greater security, but in the long term they can neither change the conditions that give rise to terrorist impulses nor eradicate the threat of terrorist attack.

The seedbed for the recruitment of large movements of extremists lies in ongoing social, economic, and political realities that can and must be recognized and addressed. This path holds the greatest promise for peace for the people of our nation and for people everywhere.

We are called to act in this time as we do in every time, renewing our own commitment to the way of Jesus Christ and to God, whose love extends to all. Offering ourselves through deeds of service and words of witness, working with our God to create a world without fear and without want, where "nation shall not lift up sword against nation, neither shall they learn war any more; but they shall all sit under their own vines and . . . fig trees, and no one shall make them afraid" (Mic. 4:3b-4a).

The Church of the Brethren. *Adapted from the General Board Resolution, October 22, 2001.*

Jesus at the National Cathedral

Heidi Regier Kreider

We are slowly beginning to grasp the significance of September 11 and what a faithful response might entail. I pondered the role of faith as I watched the religious service in the National Cathedral in Washington, D.C., on Friday, September 14, the day President Bush declared a National Day of Mourning and Prayer.

The service was a poignant and powerful experience for many, an important moment in the process of national grieving. One of the readings in that service was the Beatitudes from the Gospel of Matthew, the words of Jesus (Matt. 5:3-12). Jesus promises comfort for all who suffer, and this most certainly includes victims of the attack. As people of faith, we are compelled to show compassion for those who face enormous grief and loss. This is a time to join our community in solidarity and acts of caring.

Let this also be a reminder that people all over the nation and the world suffer terror daily, through military occupation, the threat of bombs and land mines, extreme poverty, hunger, AIDS, and environmental hazards. Does our compassion reach to them? Or does it take a crisis on American soil to stimulate sacrificial acts of caring? If God's blessing is reserved only for American victims of terrorism, then nationalism has replaced true compassion.

At the National Cathedral, religious and national symbols blurred together in subtle but powerful ways. We heard Psalm 23 sung by a children's choir while we saw images of the American flag. Military and government leaders mouthed the words of the Lord's Prayer as it was sung. The hymn "A Mighty Fortress Is Our God" was accompanied by photos of the Pentagon, now scarred and damaged, and the rubble heap that once was the World Trade Center.

What is the meaning in all this? We need a new conversation about national values and priorities, about the meaning of faith, worship, and symbols in our postmodern culture. This is a time once again to clarify the relationship between church and state. It is a time to declare our allegiance to God, who loves the people of all nations equally, and our commitment to the church that transcends all national boundaries.

As the nation seeks comfort and order in the midst of chaos, there is a drive to identify and destroy the "enemy" in order to make ourselves feel safer. National leaders have called the September 11 attack a battle between good and evil. This massive destruction of life and property was a horrific act of evil. But this does not mean that the United States is therefore morally superior, just because it was attacked. In fact, the very buildings that were attacked—the World Trade Center and the Pentagon—represent affluence and weapons that have also caused poverty, death, and suffering in the world.

The line between good and evil runs through every nation, every group of people, and every individual. This is a time to address the root causes of violence, not to perpetuate violence by seeking revenge and retaliation.

If the reading from the Gospel of Matthew had continued in Friday's service at the National Cathedral in Washington, D.C., national leaders and millions of TV-watchers around the country would have heard what else Jesus had to say. Indeed, Jesus has much to say in this context:

> You have heard that it was said, "You shall love your neighbor and hate your enemy." But I say to you, Love your enemies and pray for those who persecute you, so that you may be children of your Father in heaven; for he makes his sun rise on the evil and on the good, and sends rain on the righteous and the unrighteous. For if you love those who love you, what reward do you have? Do not even the tax collectors do the same? And if you greet only your brothers and sisters, what more are you doing than others? Do not even the Gentiles do the same? Be perfect therefore, as your heavenly Father is perfect. (Matt. 5:38-48)

We *are* far from perfect. We have no choice but to fall before God in humility and confession. We confess our participation in institutions and lifestyles that perpetuate suffering, the evil that we harbor in our own hearts, our complacency in the face of violence, and our arrogance toward those who believe differently. It is only through such repentance that we will be able to follow Jesus, love the world as God does, and discover God's strength and wisdom for the challenges ahead.

Our nation stands on the brink of war, ready to meet terrorism with an even greater show of deadly force. May God grant us the grace to meet evil with love, terror with courage, and death with the life we have in Christ.

Heidi Regier Kreider *is pastor at Bethel College Mennonite Church, North Newton, Kansas. Adapted from a sermon, September 16, 2001.*

Chapter 3

Revenge, Justice, or Forgiveness?

Searing images of people jumping from the twin towers in New York and humans crushed alive in Pennsylvania and Washington, ignited cries for revenge. Rage filled the air. "Nuke the Bastards," proclaimed roadside signs. Amid the anger, any form of retaliation would hardly balance the scales of justice.

The hunger for revenge drove twelve-year-olds to beg their mothers to let them join the army. Even some religious leaders were filled with rage. In an interview after the September 14 service at the National Cathedral, a preacher said, "We must go after them with our most lethal weapons."

The national refrain soon became, "Bring them to justice." But with the national mood boiling with anger, "bringing the terrorists to justice" really meant "kill them ASAP, by any means." "Justice" became a code word to justify retaliation through military action.

What do people of faith think should be done to those who commit such atrocities? How can religious convictions and values contribute to the search for answers? When we talk of justice, what do we really mean? What do we do with our anger and pain? Can we think about healing, forgiveness, and love when the cries for revenge are so loud? The writers in chapter 3 address these profound and troubling questions as they seek to discern how people of faith should respond.

The Clarion Call to Hate

Andy Murray

The clarion call is going up from those who urge us to hate and fear in return. But if we surrender to them the best of what makes us a people—compassion, fair play, presumption of innocence—then terror has already claimed its victory.

If we see the face of one people in the enemy and do not also see that face in the victims and in those who gave countless acts of compassion and heroism in the face of tragedy, then terror has already claimed its victory.

If we only hear reports of an "Attack on America" and do not understand that there has been an attack on humanity, then terror has already claimed its victory.

If our rage and shock over this injustice and over our vulnerability evolve into our own hatred and fear, then terror has already claimed its victory.

But if our rage over the evil done to those close to us grows into a rage against the violence done to all who suffer injustices of greed and carelessness—and if our shock over our own defenselessness becomes a profound shock over the defenselessness of the uncounted unnoticed who suffer and die daily for want of a compassionate social order—*then*, and only then, will the foundations of the true fortresses against terrorism begin to take shape in our hearts and minds.

Andy Murray directs the Baker Institute for Peace and Conflict Studies at Juniata College, Huntingdon, Pennsylvania. Adapted from an address to a vigil of 400 students, September 11, 2001.

Fire from Heaven: Jesus and Terrorism

Titus Peachey

Tension filled the air. A crowd had gathered at the edge of the Samaritan village. Their eyes were set hard and cold against Jesus, James, and John. What business did this Jewish prophet have invading their Samaritan village? Why did Jesus think he could use their village as a resting place on his way to the Jewish temple in Jerusalem? Bitter memories of historical insults and skirmishes filled their minds. The crowd grew restless. They would drive this Jewish prophet and his disciples out of their village (Luke 9:51-56).

James and John seethed as the agitated crowd formed a wall of defiance at the village entrance. Clearly these petty Samaritans didn't know whom they were dealing with. Only a few days earlier, James and John had been with Jesus on the mountain. Suddenly in a blinding blaze of light, Moses and Elijah appeared—a sure sign that Jesus' kingdom was about to break into history! It was an awesome moment, filled with mystery and power. In recent days, James and John could think of little else (Luke 9:28-36).

Now they were headed to Jerusalem. Their heads swelled with visions of thrones and councils of power, of trumpets announcing their presence, of decrees issued in their name. . . . Like children, they argued about who would be the greatest in the new kingdom (Luke 9:46-48).

But for the moment, here they were, denied and rejected outside a miserable Samaritan village. James and John gave each other a nod. This insult would not stand. The kingdom was coming. Moses, Elijah, and Jesus were with them. The power of goodness would prevail. These Samaritans would pay dearly for this. "Let us call down fire from heaven to consume them," they begged Jesus.

On September 11, four U.S. airplanes were transformed into fire from heaven, and some six thousand people, created and loved by God, were killed. A few weeks later, U.S. warplanes dropped fire from heaven on Afghanistan, killing and wounding hundreds of people, created and loved by God. Were it not for Jesus' rebuke that day in Samaria, James and John would have also turned a Samaritan village and its people into smoldering ruins with fire from heaven. The stench of death would have filled the air from the charred bodies of a people created and loved by God.

This little incident in that Samaritan village some two thousand years ago does not parallel the terror and destruction that took place on September 11, 2001. Yet what unfolded in Samaria can guide our own response to September 11 and its aftermath.

All the ingredients to justify revenge are present in the biblical story. Endorsed by two of Israel's greatest prophets, Jesus was on a mission blessed by God. The cause was just, even holy. The Samaritan rejection was an insult. Fire from heaven could avenge the insult. But Jesus rejected revenge, rebuked James and John, and moved on to another village.

Shortly after the clash at the Samaritan village, Jesus sent out seventy-two disciples to the towns and villages ahead of him (Luke 10). Jesus had already seen the enraged James and John, so he gave the disciples explicit instructions about how to respond to resistance. He told them to shake the dust from their sandals, leave the village, and warn about God's future judgment. No fire from heaven! Jesus rejected terror and the spirit of revenge (10:10-12).

The crowd was happy to hear when Jesus spoke of the judgment that unbelieving towns would receive. Yet he quickly focused on their own sins and their need for repentance. To be sure, there would be judgment. But the judgment would be greater for towns and villages in the Jewish heartland than for outlying towns (Tyre and Sidon) where Jesus had performed no miracles. Jesus' remarks were particularly scathing for Capernaum: "Did you want to lift yourself up to heaven? You will be thrown down to hell!" Even in the face of others' sins, Jesus leaves no room for self-righteousness (cf. Luke 10:13-16).

The unspeakable terrors of September 11 tempt us with self-righteousness. It is tempting, even comforting, to presume our own goodness, to equate our status as victims with innocence and purity. Indeed, those who search for economic and social connections to the events of September 11 are sometimes charged with excusing terrorism. Yet in these stories, Jesus insists that we must acknowledge our own sin. He calls for repentance because the fire from heaven is also a fire of rage within us. We want revenge, and we want it now.

Later Jesus confronts his disciples with yet another astonishing lesson in the story of the good Samaritan. Imagine the utter dismay of James and John when a Samaritan appears in Jesus' story, not as an enemy, but as a hero to emulate. It is a

Samaritan who shows compassion to the man left to die by bandits, while Jewish clerics, a priest and Levite, pass him by (Luke 10:29-37).

Jesus has just complicated his disciples' world. Those thought to be outside of God's circle of grace, are the ones who surprisingly share it. Some of those assumed to be inside the circle, have no compassion or grace to share. Among those we readily identify as villains, are also people whose compassion and mercy exceeds our own.

From our vantage point two thousand years later, it is difficult to capture the emotional shock of the Samaritan's role in Jesus' story. What if the hero in Jesus' story had been a good member of the Taliban? For those in Afghanistan and other countries who have lived under U.S. bombs, perhaps the surprising hero in this story would be "a good American."

Whatever our perspective, Jesus reminds us that we serve a God whose grace extends to all, because all of us need it. Only by learning to extend and receive God's grace across bitter human boundaries will evil ever be overcome.

These stories are not a blueprint for doing nothing in the face of terror, but a plea that we should be alert to the "fire from heaven" in our own hearts. The fire of revenge from heaven was not invented on September 11. It has afflicted the human race with untold suffering for centuries. With God's help, may we find another way.

Titus Peachey *is Director of Peace Education for Mennonite Central Committee U.S. From a sermon, November 4, 2001.*

What Do You Do with Such Pain?

Tom McGrath

"If we don't transform our pain, we will always transmit it," says Franciscan priest Richard Rohr. After the events of September 11, 2001, such transformation has become all the more daunting, yet all the more necessary if we are to survive as a species, and if we are to be faithful to our God. A lot of the world is in pain. A lot of the world still transmits pain.

Some groups enter into elaborate dances with their enemies and obsessively keep transmitting pain to each other in ever higher doses. Vengeance becomes more real to them than the taste of a lover's kiss or the tender breath of a newborn baby. Brilliant minds, strong wills, and bitter and wounded souls plan and execute ever more nefarious ways of inflicting pain. This dance has been going on ever since humans crafted weapons as some of their first tools.

A few months ago, newspapers showed photos of terrified schoolgirls in Northern Ireland being pelted with bricks on the way to school. Their tormentors justified such heinous actions because the older brothers and cousins of these schoolgirls roam the neighborhoods, setting off bombs and spreading their own terror. And so it goes.

I'm thinking about the cries of Palestinians and the cries of Israelis, both so deep and heartfelt, as yet more of their family members die. Each side recites an endless list of occasions for their pain. And that propels them to leave the negotiating tables and transmit more pain. And so it goes.

I'm thinking about the Serbs and the Bosnians. The Iraqis and the Kurds. The Tutsis and the Hutus. The Indonesians and the East Timorese. And so it goes.

"It is natural for our shock to give way to anger," said Bishop Walter Sullivan days after the attack on the World Trade Towers. "We must be careful that it does not give way to vengeance." After repeatedly seeing that Boeing 767 plow into the South Tower, my mind gave way to thoughts of vengeance. I was conjuring up cruel vendettas. In that frame of mind, it would be easy to enter into the dance of death, to begin the long downward spiral that has no end.

In the face of that bleak prospect, Christian hope dares to suggest that there is another choice beyond revenge: it is reconciliation. Just saying this, I hear the chorus of angry voices accusing me of naïveté, complicity with the enemy, foolishness, and treason. But Jesus, who we claim has the words of eternal life, directs us unequivocally to love our enemies and do good to those who hate us (cf. Luke 6:27).

I'm not suggesting absolving the criminals or forgoing the administration of justice. But while we prepare to defend ourselves from a real and ever-growing threat, our preparations should not simply be defensive and certainly not include retaliation against innocent people we assume are guilty by association. We must also begin the difficult work of seeking reconciliation with Muslims around the world.

Osama bin Laden gained popularity among many Muslims for a reason, because he strongly articulates grievances his coreligionists feel. He taps into their pain, puts a twisted religious spin on it, and whips it into violent frenzy. Bin Laden is not the first world leader to use this tactic, and he won't be the last. Certainly he must be brought to justice.

But what are we doing about communicating with and connecting to the Muslims whose pain he exploits? What do we know of the grievances of these people we dismiss so easily? Before committing the mortal sin of "bombing them back to the Stone Age," wouldn't it be wise to examine the reasons for their intense pain and hate? In honest humility, wouldn't it be wise to see what our part might be in that?

I hear people say, "Be realistic." But what is more realistic than acknowledging that the evil does not exist just "out there," that it also exists within me. It's just as dangerous in me as it is "out there." Right now, the most realistic thing I can think of is that we stand at the edge of a slippery slope. Forces of evil are taunting and daring us to slide on down.

In the face of death, we ought to seek a wisdom that can lead us out of the valley of death. We must seek justice and also reconciliation. That will take *more* strength, courage, and love of country than simply thumping our chests and vowing to "bring these people down." Seeking reconciliation is not only the way of Jesus; it also is our only hope to build a life worth living for those who will come after us.

Tom McGrath *is the author of* Raising Faith-Filled Kids: Ordinary Opportunities to Nurture Spirituality at Home *(Loyola Press). Adapted from an essay in the* U.S. Catholic, *November 2001.*

Choking on Ashes

Kevin Clarke

Can justice, not retribution, be served in response to America's worst terrorist attack?

I grew up in a family thick with cops and firemen, in a New York suburb peopled by cops and firemen. So it was with a special dread that I watched a churning cloud of dust, debris, and choking ash envelope people running for their lives in lower Manhattan on September 11. I knew a fear that had haunted my childhood would come home that night as a terrible reality to hundreds of New York families.

Like millions of others, I watched each terrible development through that awful morning, between fruitless attempts to call home. I contacted one brother just as the second tower collapsed, stunning us both into silence. He was frantic and furious and ready to fight somebody, but he and his family were safe. Another brother was out of town, and a sister and parents were home. One cousin, a firefighter, called to say he was okay and on his way to the crash site. Everyone was safe, no one was safe, and a world of suffering was just opening up to my friends and neighbors in New York.

These have been terrible days, and more terrible days may lie ahead. We are eager for justice, ready to strike out. Even the pacifists among us struggle to restrain a subterranean yearning for violent revenge for such an evil act.

But in this instance it is possible to do worse than no

good. It is possible to build the foundation for only more bloodshed. Before we act, we need to be still. We need to understand the anger that compelled these men, men with fathers, friends, brothers, and cousins just like me, men who nurtured such hatred that they finally became capable of this appalling gesture of cold-blooded malice.

Otherwise, the events of September 11 will one day be remembered as only a wretched footnote in the centuries-old conflict between the Western and the Islamic worlds, a conflict that drives a colorful history but takes us nowhere but to more despair and anguish. The bitter truth—bitter, because retribution beckons our wounded spirit with its false promises—may be that the most rational and practical response to this provocation comes not at the end of a gun but at the end of a handshake.

By the time you read this, our nation may have completed a retaliation for the terrible suffering of September 11. On that day, I tried to pray, but I was too numb and too defeated to pray. The words would not come to me.

Here is my prayer now: Lord, we call out for justice. Grant us justice, not revenge. Lord, we have terrible power within our reach; grant us the strength to wield our power with wisdom, with mercy. Help us to comprehend what seems incomprehensible. Lord, we do not want to see another day like September 11, nor do we wish to condemn our children to relive it. Allow us the grace to be the generation to break this cycle of violence, this history of hate. Let us not leave it to our sons and daughters to confront again that awful spectacle of dust and debris and choking ash.

Kevin Clarke is a Contributing Editor to the U.S. Catholic. *Adapted from an article in that periodical, November 2001.*

Called to Another Way

Frank T. Griswold

Our president has vowed to hunt down and punish those responsible for these depraved and wicked acts. Many are speaking of revenge. Never has it been clearer to me than in this moment that people of faith, by virtue of the gospel and the mission of the church, are called to be about peace and the transformation of the human heart, beginning with our own. I am not immune to emotions of rage and revenge, but I know that acting on them only perpetuates the very violence I pray will be dissipated and overcome.

Yes, those responsible must be found and punished for their evil and disregard for human life. Yet through the heart of this violence, we are called to another way. May our response be to engage with all our hearts and minds and strength in God's project of transforming the world into a garden, a place of peace, where swords become plowshares and spears become pruning hooks (cf. Isa. 2:4; Mic. 4:3).

The Most Rev. Frank T. Griswold is Presiding Bishop and Primate, The Episcopal Church, USA. Adapted from a letter, September 11, 2001.

Overcoming Evil with Good

Bob Gross

Nothing that happened on September 11 changes anything about the Christian faith. The will of God, as we know it through the example and teachings of Jesus Christ, is the same today. It may be more difficult for us to hear, but the call of God on our lives has not changed.

One of the things we have been hearing is *rage*. We are outraged when we think of the terrible things that have happened and all the lives that have been lost. But what will we do with our rage?

The Scripture says, "Be angry but do not sin" (Eph. 4:26; Ps. 4:4; James 1:19-20). It's one thing to be outraged, but it's another thing to act out of rage. It's one thing to feel hatred toward those who took so many lives on September 11. It's another thing to dwell in hatred. "Be angry but do not sin."

I believe that part of our anger and rage—maybe a big part—comes from our fear. We feel so vulnerable. We are afraid in a new way. The most dangerous thing we can do is to fight violence with violence. That's why Jesus and Paul say, Do not try to fight evil with evil (Matt. 5; Rom. 12:17; 1 Thess. 5:15). They understand the power of evil.

When we try to fight evil with evil, we are overcome by evil. We are overcome by evil not when violence happens to us, but when we choose to respond with evil.

I have friends who lost loved ones to murder. One of those

loved ones murdered was Bill Bosler, pastor of Miami First Church of the Brethren. One day just before Christmas, Bill and his daughter SueZann were in the parsonage in Miami when a knock came at the door. Bill opened the door to a young man he had met once before at the church. But this time was different.

The young man, James Campbell, had come to rob the house, to get money for drugs. He started stabbing Bill. SueZann came to defend her father, and James turned his attack on her. When James thought both of them were dead, he ransacked the house, looking for money and valuables, then left. SueZann was not dead. She eventually recovered, but Bill never regained consciousness.

When he was attacked and killed by James Campbell, Bill was not overcome by evil. They would have been overcome by evil if his family had devoted themselves to hating James Campbell, if they had done everything they could to make sure that he died in Florida's execution chamber.

While SueZann was still in the hospital, recovering from brain surgery, prosecutors started talking to her about the death penalty for James. As she recovered and started to think clearly, she began to say, "Wait! That's not what my father would want. That's not what our family wants."

I remember SueZann carrying a Bible to every meeting and conference she attended, and asking people to sign their names in it. She was going to give that Bible to James some day. She wanted him to know what kind of man he had killed, and to know the peace of Christ that her dad knew.

Throughout the long legal process, while the prosecution was seeking the death penalty for James, she was trying to save his life. One day in court she was able to look him in the eye and tell him that she forgave him. In large part because of

SueZann's efforts, James Campbell will not die in Florida's execution chamber. He will probably spend the rest of his days in prison, but his life has been spared.

"If your enemies are hungry, feed them; if they are thirsty, give them something to drink; for by doing this you will heap burning coals on their heads" (Rom. 12:20). This is what SueZann has done. The "coals of fire" she has heaped on James by being kind to him have caused him to think about his life and about her Christian witness.

When the planes hit the World Trade Center and the Pentagon, and so many people died, our nation was not, at that point, overcome by evil. I think the real danger of that is in what happens in response.

Someone asked an expert on terrorism about the mind-set of the persons who hijacked those planes. She explained that the terrorist mentality is one that says, "We are totally good, our cause is totally just, and we are justified in taking any action against our enemy, who is totally evil."

As I listened, I suddenly realized, That's what we are hearing from many of our national leaders. It's what we are hearing at the local coffee shops. It is the language of holy war. And this is the real power of evil. Evil has the power, if we let it, to turn us away from God. "Do not be overcome by evil." "Do not repay anyone evil for evil" (Rom. 12:21, 17). If you want to defeat evil, use the power of good.

Right now our nation—and each one of us—has the same choice SueZann had. We have a choice about whether to be overcome by evil, or to follow Jesus in transforming evil with good. Right now, we are to love our enemies and do good to those who persecute us. We are never to repay evil for evil, but instead to overcome evil with good. This witness has never been more needed in our world.

Please pray that we will remain faithful. Pray that we will hear and answer God's call. It will not be an easy path, but it is the one Jesus chose. It will not be an easy path, but God will be with us every step of the way.

Bob Gross *is Co-Executive Director of On Earth Peace Assembly, New Windsor, Maryland. Adapted from a sermon, September 16, 2001.*

Not in Our Son's Name

Phyllis and Orlando Rodriguez

Our son, Greg, is among the many missing from the World Trade Center attack.

Since we first heard the news, we have shared moments of grief, comfort, hope, despair, and fond memories with his wife, the two families, our friends and neighbors, his loving colleagues at Cantor Fitzgerald/ESpeed, and all the grieving families that daily meet at the Pierre Hotel.

We see our hurt and anger reflected among everybody we meet. We cannot pay attention to the daily flow of news about this disaster. But we read enough of the news to sense that our government is heading in the direction of violent revenge, with the prospect of sons, daughters, parents, and friends in distant lands dying, suffering, and nursing further grievances against us.

It is not the way to go. It will not avenge our son's death. Not in our son's name.

Our son died a victim of an inhuman ideology. Our actions should not serve the same purpose. Let us grieve. Let us reflect and pray. Let us think about a rational response that brings real peace and justice to our world. But let us not as a nation add to the inhumanity of our times.

Phyllis and Orlando Rodriguez, *in a letter to the* New York Times.

Dear President Bush:

Our son is one of the victims of Tuesday's attack on the World Trade Center. We read about your response in the last few days and about the solutions from both Houses, giving you undefined power to respond to the terror attacks.

Your response to this attack does not make us feel better about our son's death. It makes us feel worse. We feel that our government is using our son's memory as a justification to cause suffering for other sons and parents in other lands.

It is not the first time a person in your position has been given unlimited power and come to regret it. This is not the time for empty gestures to make us feel better. It is not the time to act like bullies. We urge you to think about how our government can develop peaceful, rational solutions to terrorism, not sinking us to the inhuman level of terrorists.

Phyllis and Orlando Rodriguez, *in a letter sent to the White House.*

Family Asks for No Innocent Blood

Andrew Bushe

The Irish brothers of New York terror victim Ruth McCourt and her four-year-old daughter, Juliana, who both died in a plane that crashed into the World Trade Center, have pleaded for no innocent blood to be spilled in revenge for the atrocity.

From Dublin, Ireland, John and Mark Clifford made an emotional appeal for measured justice and just retribution.

"We want people to restrain themselves from the gut reaction of wanting retribution," said Mark.

"For one child to die in Juliana's retribution would kill us as a family. We say, please, please don't kill innocents. Focus your energy. Bring these people to justice. Do not kill for the sake of killing. Juliana was a beautiful child, and Ruth stood for color in life, not the black-and-white scenario a lot of people live with, either friend or foe."

John said it was appalling to think of an innocent barefoot Afghan child dying as a result of the atrocity. "We must show restraint. Innocence must be preserved. What kind of legacy have we left our kids? Justice must be done. People must be accountable for what they have done. But don't involve the innocent."

Andrew Bushe, reporting in the Irish Echo, *week of September 19-25, 2001.*

A Widow's Plea for Nonviolence

Amber Amundson

My husband, Craig Scott Amundson of the U.S. Army, lost his life in the line of duty at the Pentagon on September 11 as the world looked on in horror and disbelief.

Losing my twenty-eight-year-old husband and father of our two young children is a terrible and painful experience.

His death is also part of an immense national loss, and I am comforted by knowing so many share my grief.

But because I have lost Craig as part of this historic tragedy, my anguish is compounded exponentially by fear that this death will be used to justify new violence against other innocent victims.

I have heard angry rhetoric by some Americans, including many of our nation's leaders, who advise a heavy dose of revenge and punishment. To those leaders, I would like to make clear that my family and I take no comfort in your words of rage. If you choose to respond to this incomprehensible brutality by perpetuating violence against other innocent human beings, you may not do so in the name of justice for my husband.

Your words and acts of revenge only amplify our family's suffering, deny us the dignity of remembering our loved one in a way that would have made him proud, and mock his vision of America as a peacemaker in the world community.

My husband enlisted in the army and was proud to serve

his county. He was a patriotic American and a citizen of the world. Craig believed that by working from within the military system, he could help to maintain the military focus on peacekeeping and strategic planning, to prevent violence and war. For the last two years, Craig drove to the Pentagon with a VISUALIZE WORLD PEACE bumper sticker on his car. This was not empty rhetoric or contradictory to him, but part of his dream. He believed his role in the army could further the cause of peace throughout the world.

Craig would not have wanted a violent response to avenge his death. And I cannot see how good can come out of it. We cannot solve violence. Mohandas Gandhi said, "An eye for an eye only makes the whole world blind." We will no longer be able to see that we hold the light of liberty if we are blinded by vengeance, anger, and fear. I ask our nation's leaders not to take the path that leads to more widespread hatreds and makes my husband's death just one more in an unending spiral of killing.

I call on our national leaders to find the courage to respond to this incomprehensible tragedy by breaking the cycle of violence. I call on them to marshal this great nation's skills and resources, to lead a worldwide dialogue on freedom from terror and hate.

I do not know how to begin making a better world: I do believe it must be done, and I believe it is our leaders' responsibility to find a way. I urge them to take up this challenge and respond to our nation's tragedy and my personal tragedy with a new start that gives us hope for a peaceful global community.

Amber Amundson, wife of the late Craig Scott Amundson, writing to the Chicago Tribune, *September 25, 2001. Copyright 2001, Chicago Tribune Company. All rights reserved. Used with permission.*

To Embrace the Enemy: Is Reconciliation Possible?

Miroslav Volf

In New York City, while terrorists destroyed the World Trade Center and thousands of innocent lives, Volf was nearby, speaking at the Annual International Prayer Breakfast at the United Nations building on reconciling with our enemies. Christianity Today *senior news writer Tony Carnes spoke to him about terrorism and forgiveness.*

When did you discover that the World Trade Center had been attacked?

After my talk, as I was leaving the UN building, some of the UN personnel informed us that there had been a major terrorist attack. As I walked out to Grand Central Station, I could see a large cloud of dust in the distance.

Were you afraid?

I felt very strange. I had been inside talking about reconciliation with our enemies at the same time that a terrorist attack was taking place and the World Trade Center towers were collapsing. You have to understand: I come from a country that suffered comparatively much greater damage—where one third of the land was captured and whole cities were leveled. Near my own home city, just one town, Vukovar, was completely destroyed, and 30,000 people were either killed or driven out. Out of a population of 4.5 million, we had about a million refugees. Still, I was horrified and shocked by what happened here.

As many as 5,000 people may have been killed as a result of the attack on the World Trade Center. Does this kind of atrocity cause you to second-guess your ideas about reconciliation with one's enemies?

One of the points in my talk at the UN was that we, as Christians, must develop a will to embrace and be reconciled with our enemy. This will to embrace is absolutely unconditional. There is no imaginable deed that should take a person outside our will to embrace him, because there is no imaginable deed that can take a person out of God's will to embrace humanity—which is what I think is inscribed in big letters in the narrative of the cross of Christ.

A tragedy like September 11 comes close to the sort of offense that one could imagine would put its perpetrators beyond our will to embrace them, but it does not. And it does not simply because Christ already died for all of us.

But reconciliation is the last thing on the minds of most Americans—including Christians. We are angry.

The first thought on many of our minds was that such vicious acts demand revenge. When I realized what happened, I felt a sense of shock and grief for the loss of life and the major disruption that had taken place. But then I felt we needed to go after them, that they needed to pay.

Is it wrong to feel that way?

On one level, there will be a gut reaction, a sense of rage. Rage is a natural first response. It is also an appropriate response if we do it before the God of infinite love and justice. That is how I read the imprecatory Psalms, like Psalm 137, which pronounce blessing on those who seize and dash the Babylonian little ones against the rock. Those words may sound vengeful. But what is significant is that, this being a ritual prayer, the psalmist is giving his anger over to God. In the same way, we need to bring our rage before God and the cross of Christ.

Ultimately, however, we cannot leave it at the gut reaction. There must be a Christian response. And as Christians, the will to embrace and forgive our enemy must be unconditional. How do we respond as Christians, not simply as human beings or as patriots who have legitimate feelings of being aggrieved and assaulted? This is the important question. And the answer lies in reconciliation.

What about justice?

Divine grace does not preclude justice being done. The naming of the deeds as evil and the protection of those who are innocent is extraordinarily important. But none of these things means we should not also seek to forgive the offender and reconcile with the offender. We can never close the door to reconciliation, and all our actions must be directed toward the goal of reconciliation. Just reconciliation, of course, because justice is an integral part of reconciliation.

What if the other party—your enemy—sees you as a cancer on the world, as many Muslim extremists view Americans?

The perspective of the other person may not be the correct one and probably is a profoundly skewed one. Enmity, especially strong enmity, has the effect of skewing perspectives on others. However, there might be questions of justice between nations that are at stake here, too. We would do well to use this occasion as a nation to ask, "What would cause a person or group of individuals to see us in a way you describe and commit such an act?" Many people from outside this nation, rightly or wrongly, think of the United States as this huge giant with economic and military prowess that steps on the toes of smaller nations. That perspective is, on the whole, not correct, but some of it may be true.

For any victim, particularly us Americans, it is difficult to see ourselves through the eyes of our offender. But for any victim it is the most salutary thing to do. Why was I perceived this way? Why did they act toward me in this way? This in no way justifies the hatred of their behavior toward us, especially when thousands of innocent people are killed. But the sheer exercise of examining our own actions and attitudes can be fruitful, and it is indeed essential if we are to reconcile and live in peace with justice.

President Bush has suggested that bringing Osama bin Laden and other terrorist leaders to justice may require killing them. Would that be just?

We have to protect ourselves from the possibility of such an event happening again. That's easier when the evildoer can be caught and restrained. But religious terrorism and suicide bombings are not like other crimes. If you are certain they would repeat the act, trying to stop them and in the process possibly killing them may be required. I think it would be analogous to the situation with Hitler's Germany.

I have always felt that Christians like Dietrich Bonhoeffer, who plotted an assassination of Hitler, had the right perspective on such acts. Bonhoeffer was convinced that he was doing the right thing, even though doing the right thing entailed doing the wrong thing. He was doing a right thing for which he felt he had to repent. He was doing the right wrong thing.

Taking a life is always the wrong thing. The choice Bonhoeffer had was doing the lesser of the evils. However, the fact that one has to do evil and chooses the lesser one doesn't mean it becomes not evil. He must still repent of his sin. The self-righteousness with which we go after those who have assaulted us and the absence of any sense that we ourselves are implicated in their act, deeply troubles me.

Do you agree with the rhetoric of war that has been applied to this event?

There has been much talk about "hunting down" and "punishing" the terrorists. That is very dangerous language. Animals are hunted down. Such language serves to take the perpetrators out of the community of our species: "They are the barbarians and animals, and we are good and decent people." We must work to find out who did it and, in a carefully qualified sense, bring those people to justice. But we shouldn't speak in a way that debases their humanity. Such language seems to put the perpetrator beyond redemption.

How can there be a genuine reconciliation between terrorist and victim when both are dead? And how can there be an embrace when we don't know who did this?

Christians believe that there will be a judgment day at the end. It is my belief that on that day justice will be done and there will be a reconciliation between those who have profoundly injured one another. My Yale colleague Professor Carlos Eire sometimes visits his relatives in a small community of Cuban immigrants near Chicago. Not long ago, a pious Catholic woman there asked him, "Is it possible for Fidel Castro to be in heaven?"

Professor Eire told her that the Christian faith teaches that nobody is beyond the pale of redemption. It is possible for Castro to end up in heaven. There was dead silence. Then she said, "Well, I wouldn't want to be in heaven. I can't imagine a heaven in which I would live with Fidel Castro." This woman could not fathom the scandalous truth that no one—not even our mortal enemies—is beyond divine grace.

Many events in this world remain hidden in deep obscurity. We don't know who all the perpetrators of this evil act are. We don't know exactly how to seek real justice. That is why there will be a last judgment. Generally, when people talk of the last judgment, they say it is a horrible day.

But the final judgment is good news, certainly good news to the victims, and also good news to the perpetrators, since the judgment will be rendered not only by a just Judge who sees and knows all things, but also by the Judge who has given his life for the salvation of the world. Christ who died on the cross is the same Christ who will sit on the judgment seat and who is going to render the judgment, the judgment of justice and of grace. He is the reason why forgiveness and reconciliation are possible.

Miroslav Volf is Professor of Theology at Yale Divinity School. Born in Croatia, he lived in Communist Yugoslavia and witnessed ethnic tensions and war between the Croats and Serbs. His book Exclusion and Embrace: A Theological Exploration of Identity, Otherness, and Reconciliation *explores the theological implications of reconciliation. Adapted from an interview in* Christianity Today.

Forgiveness? Now?

Donald W. Shriver Jr.

The events of September 11 test our American Christian ability to demonstrate moral judgment without an instinct for revenge, an empathy for our enemies without sympathy for their crimes, and a hope that we can eventually find ways to reconcile with them. This complex combination amounts to a definition of forgiveness. We should be devoting a lot of time and energy to coping with the complexities of forgiveness as they relate to our immediate and long-term relation to the world of Islam.

But in the midst of this crisis, we can also talk about forgiveness prematurely. Some years ago, a young man of thirteen murdered a young man of sixteen as the latter was coming out of the Corpus Christi Catholic Church. The victim's father was a practicing Catholic and a parole officer. After the funeral service, he said to a reporter, "My faith in religion is one of forgiveness, turn the other cheek. It's what one has to do as a Christian, but it's not easy to do."

I remember admiring this man's simultaneous struggle with grief and his duty to forgive. But I could not help thinking that the church that had taught him the centrality of forgiveness should relieve him of that obligation for the time being. Grief must have its day—or its year. Moral outrage too. And a struggle against the natural precipitate of rage infused with grief: hatred.

Islamic theologians make a distinction between the greater jihad and the lesser jihad. The Arabic word means "struggle," and contrary to what non-Muslims might assume, the lesser struggle is the external, sometimes militant one. The greater struggle is the internal effort to conform oneself to the will of God. Speaking as one New Yorker and one Christian among many, I am aware that in this current national crisis, I have to struggle to relate my grief and anger to my potential for hate. Perhaps I am confessing that this theologian needs pastoral care.

My guess is that we all need it. We are not likely to respond favorably to sermons telling us that we should leap to forgiveness of our enemies while they are still intending, in the next round of terror, to kill Americans for being American. Why should we even speak of forgiveness while an enemy shows no disposition to discontinue threatening our lives or to repent of doing so? Nor can we accommodate, just now, too heavy a burden of calling our nation to repentance for our undoubted sins against too many of the world's poor.

Yet if we were to postpone indefinitely all thought of forgiveness or repentance, we would be abandoning our commission to live and act as a people of faith in a world where we are supposed to be salt and light (Matt. 5:13-16). A resistance to hate has to rank high in the inmost depths of our souls as a current spiritual priority. Hiding inside of us is a deep capacity for hate.

I cannot speak for other American Christians, but I for one find myself praying the Lord's Prayer with new fear and trembling. The exclamation "My God!" had become so popular that Americans forgot that the words are a first-person address. On September 11, New Yorkers remembered. People prayed that day in their own stumbling ways. Some of us prayed the Lord's Prayer. I like what A. B. Bruce wrote years ago: "The Lord's Prayer is not merely for heroes, but for the timid, the inexperienced. The teacher is considerate, and allows time for reaching the heights of heroism."

So it is with me. I need, in particular, the petitions for forgiveness and deliverance from evil, including the temptation to return evil for evil. If you will so deliver me, Lord, I may learn again to forgive as I am forgiven.

And for climbing toward that height of spiritual heroism, Lord, I need some time.

Donald W. Shriver Jr., *President Emeritus of Union Theological Seminary (N.Y.), is author of* An Ethic for Enemies: Forgiveness in Politics. *Copyright 2001 Christian Century Foundation. Adapted with permission from the October 24-31, 2001,* Christian Century. *Subscriptions: $49/yr. from P.O. Box 378, Mt. Morris, IL 61054.*

What Comes After the Anger?

Terry Mattingly

Terry Anderson thought he had conquered his anger at the terrorists who locked him away for 2,545 days.

The Associated Press veteran had traveled back to Lebanon to make a documentary. He met with officials of Hezbollah. It was hard, but he did it.

Then an image on his giant-screen television brought it all back. Anderson was watching a routine news interview with a politician in Beirut when he recognized his voice. This was the man the hostages called "the boss," in their shadowy world of blindfolds and secret prisons.

"I knew that voice. We had to listen to him day after day. He was in charge," Anderson said this week at St. Andrews School in Boca Raton, Florida. "And there he was in my living room, larger than life, on my television screen in Ohio. I'm watching him and listening to him and I'm thinking, 'You bastard! I am still angry, because you did that to me.'"

"That surprised me. It surprised me that it was still buried in there someplace."

On September 11, Anderson was stunned and horrified all over again.

Anderson has paid his dues. He knows all about terrorism, nationalism, religious fanaticism, and the other isms that haunt the Middle East. He knows more than anyone could want to know about the agonizing path that broken people will have to walk after the events in New York City, Washington (D.C.), and rural Pennsylvania.

But Anderson isn't sure he can grasp the pain felt by those who lost loved ones on September 11, even after his years as a hostage and as a war correspondent. Anderson said he isn't even sure what to call what happened on that day. "Terrorism" is being radically redefined.

"These terrorists are not asking for anything. There are no demands. They simply want to destroy," he said. "There is no question of negotiation. They are anarchists. It used to be that terror had political aims. They can't really have any expectations that they can damage us in any lasting way. This is terror for the sake of terrorizing people."

Anderson's testimony on faith and forgiveness was scheduled before the bombings. Above all, he said he considers himself blessed. He is thankful for his life, marriage, family, and work as a writer and teacher. He said he is thankful for the faith that helped him stay sane in his chains, locked away with a circle of brothers that included a Catholic priest and a biblical scholar.

But this is a hard time to preach about the power of forgiveness. "Right now, I don't think the people who lost loved ones at the World Trade Center even want to *hear* the word 'forgiveness.' They are still grieving, as we all are, as a nation," he said. "When I speak about forgiveness, I am speaking totally about my personal experience, my own feelings, and my own search. I cannot speak for anyone else."

During the decade since his release, the tenets of his faith have brought him pain as well as comfort. It's hard to get past the words that are "right there on the very first page of our contract [with God]," he said. "That's the place where it says, 'Forgive us our trespasses, as we forgive those who trespass against us'" (Matt. 6:12, *Book of Common Prayer*).

Anderson said his wife once described the lessons they have learned this way: "If you want the joy, you can't have the anger."

What does this mean for the nation? Anderson is convinced America can seek security without surrendering its values of freedom. The free world can demand justice for Osama bin Laden, without making decisions rooted in a thirst for revenge.

"The people who kidnapped me, just like those who committed this terrible atrocity, are not sorry today. They are not asking for forgiveness. No, forgiveness is about what is in me. Hatred and anger are terribly debilitating. They are even soul-destroying, I think, when they are righteous.

"We have every reason to be terribly angry at those people," he said. "They need to be punished. But anger will lead us, I think, into places where we do not want to go."

Terry Mattingly (www.tmatt.net) is Professor of Mass Media and Religion at Palm Beach Atlantic College, Florida. Adapted from his weekly column for the Scripps Howard News Service.

Feeding the Gentle Wolf

Nancy Good Sider

A Native American grandfather was talking to his grandson about how he felt about a tragedy. The older man said, "I feel as if I have two wolves fighting in my heart. One wolf is the vengeful, angry, violent one. The other wolf is the loving, gentle, compassionate one."

"Which wolf will win the fight in your heart?" asked the grandson.

"The one I feed," replied the grandfather.

This story highlights the conflicting feelings—the wolves—that emerge from tragedy, and makes the startling suggestion that we need to attend to both of them. Both wolves are real and alive following violent trauma. The challenge is how to heal the fury and rage of the one wolf, and feed the love and mercy of the other.

This certainly is the task faced by all of us following September 11 and especially by those directly affected. How do we begin to heal after such a terrible nightmare? Is it even possible to think of forgiveness?

Church leaders in New York especially have pondered these questions. Even six weeks after the attack, many people near ground zero were still in shock and disbelief that the towers were gone. The air continued to fill with smoke, like an incinerator that never stopped burning. The odor was constant, and people jumped at the slightest sudden noise.

Many still had no phone service and found it difficult to get basic food items. Many lost jobs and face an uncertain future. To cope, many remain in a state of denial, unable to face the enormous destruction surrounding them. Still others feel guilty that they and their families survived when so many of their co-workers and friends perished or lost family.

The healing process from intense trauma is a slow, arduous journey. People need time to grieve, cry, and be angry. There is no quick fix, no laser treatments for emotional and spiritual pain. Often the only path to healing leads through the pain.

The church can be a place of hospitality for this journey, a place where patience and generosity abound. As Henri Nouwen explained in *Reaching Out*, "Hospitality is not to change the people, but to offer them space where change can take place." People need a safe place to grieve and to face the horror of their experience.

In the initial stages, people tend to deny or suppress their grief and fears. They are often angry and desire retaliation. Many tell their story frequently and may plan some act of aggression. Why let go and move on? Why forgive or even think about it? The pain, violation, or injustice is so great that the main impulse—which can stay for months and years— is to get even. This is a crucial, first stage of healing. In *Trauma and Recovery*, Judith Herman notes that the first task toward recovery is the establishment of the survivor's safety. "No other (healing) work can possibly succeed if safety has not been adequately secured."

The survivor then needs to find some answers to the questions of why to move on. Sometimes we need to go round and round the inner circle of revenge until we are certain that we have to—and gradually choose to—take another kind of healing path. We discover that nothing new or good under the sun is in the inner circle of anger, revenge, and hatred. We actually discover that we have become like the enemy. The bitterness is destructive for the self as well as the other. The outer circle toward healing seems so unnatural until we realize that reactions of revenge, arising so instinctively in the inner circle, are not good for us or our communities.

For healing to progress, people need to move out of the circle of revenge and stop "feeding the vengeful wolf." This means fully facing and mourning one's losses, confronting one's fears, and finding some measure of acceptance that allows for letting go of the bitterness and anger. For some survivors, it is helpful to address the perpetrator(s) of the harm, to ask questions, and to express their deep pain.

Healing is also a process that entails being patient with oneself and others through the journey. Trauma healing is not one-directional or linear. Like the grief stages, a person does not follow a tidy progression from one stage to the next. Trauma healing, like trauma itself, is messy, confusing, intense, and overwhelming. Persons often jump around, surviving the best they can. Some may even move to the outer circle toward healing, only to find themselves again in the circle of revenge.

Thus healing calls for decisions as well—decisions to move toward healing or remain in the react, revenge, and get-even circle. A survivor of the Bosnian war, Amela Puljek-Shank, recalls how helpful it was to realize that she could choose how to respond. "I began to see that I had a choice to remain in the inner circle of anger and wanting to do violence, or to move toward trauma healing. A choice to heal rather than to hate and kill. A choice to possibly become a healthy individual again. A choice to take some steps to move back home after displacement—home to my spirit, my body, my homeland."

Finally, survivors need to discover a way to remember and tell their story. We know that "forgive and forget" does not work and actually layers on more trauma. Rather, survivors need to discover ways to remember and move on so that they can begin to live with the trauma story differently.

In the months and years ahead, all of us will be walking this recovery journey at some level. Let us help each other acknowledge the pain and the rage but also find ways to feed the wolf that will lead to healing and transformation.

Nancy Good Sider is a Professor in the Conflict Transformation Program of Eastern Mennonite University (Harrisonburg, Va.). Adapted from reflections, at a Church World Service Interfaith Trauma Response Workshop, New York City, October 27-28, 2001, and from her article on the website www.emu.edu.

What Kind of Justice?

Linda Gehman Peachey

Following the attacks of September 11, President Bush talked of hunting down terrorists and destroying them—finding those responsible, "bringing them to justice." What kind of justice did he mean? While some of this language contained hints of holy war, these images are also consistent with a justice of retribution. This means that when people cause pain, an equal measure of pain should be meted out; when they break a law, they should be punished.

Our current criminal justice system is based on this model. The state takes primary responsibility for administering justice, and the legal system is built around determining who is guilty and what the punishment should be. The immediate victims are often removed from the picture, with little opportunity to give input, except as witnesses to the crime. Also, little encouragement or opportunity is given to offenders to express remorse or to understand the impact of their crime.

Another approach to justice began to emerge in the early 1970s. A visionary probation officer in Ontario, Canada, searched for a better way to hold accountable two young men who had vandalized twenty-two properties. What would happen, he wondered, if they could meet the victims, apologize, and work out a restitution plan directly with the people affected by their crime? The judge agreed to the idea. With supervision, the young men visited most of these homes and worked out restitution plans. Within months, they made repayment.

As people elsewhere experimented with this process, they began thinking about justice in new ways, eventually giving birth to the current restorative justice movement. Restorative justice sees crime primarily as a violation of people and relationships, creating obligations to make things right. As Dan Van Ness says, "Crime is a wound, justice is healing." This model of justice insists that the offender, the victim, and the community should all have central roles in finding solutions that promote repair and restoration.

The state still has a legitimate role to provide protection and, when necessary, place dangerous individuals in a secure environment where they cannot harm others or themselves. But this role should not eclipse the involvement of those directly involved in the crime.

Restorative justice often brings victims and offenders together with third-party facilitators, who help the parties talk about the crime and its harm, and work out a restitution agreement. This process gives victims an opportunity to ask questions that can be answered only by the offender, to share directly the pain and anguish the crime has caused, and to seek restitution meaningful to them. It also encourages the offender to take responsibility for the crime, to share remorse, and to understand how the restitution relates to the crime.

This process has been used most frequently with juvenile offenders who commit property crimes such as vandalism or theft. Sometimes it is used in place of the normal court procedures and sanctions; at other times, it occurs alongside the current system. Over the past decade, the model has also been adapted and used as well in situations of severe crime.

A number of states now administer programs that assist victims who would like to meet their offender. As Kay Pranis, a restorative justice planner with the Minnesota Department of Corrections, writes, "In places as diverse as Ontario, Texas, Minnesota, and Oregon, victims and offenders have come together to deal with cases of severe violence. They have found a nonviolent way to affirm the wrongness of the actions, acknowledge the depth of the pain, and shift their orientation toward hope."

Pranis describes the experience of one woman, whose only son was murdered. "The only person from whom she felt unconditional love in her life was taken from her in an act of violence. After years of hate and a desire to hurt in return, she met face to face with the perpetrator. She wished to confront him, to make him face the harm he had done. In the sharing of woundedness in their face-to-face dialog, she responded to him with love, and she experienced a sense of peace and justice that she had not felt before in her hate and desire for revenge."

Can restorative justice work in situations of great oppression, fueled by centuries of ethnic conflict? The Truth and Reconciliation Commission in South Africa was one attempt to apply this model on a more systemic level. Yet, more needs to be done. There are no clear and easy answers.

And there are no quick solutions that can address the enormous harms caused by the events of September 11. Restorative justice does not promise the swift punishment than can be meted out by the punitive model of justice. Still, it seeks a way to hold perpetrators more accountable, give victims a voice, and more effectively address the harm that was done. In the end, finding a way to apply these longer-term concerns to difficult international situations could bring greater security, even from terrorists.

Linda Gehman Peachey is a freelance writer of Lancaster, Pennsylvania. For additional reading, see Kay Pranis, "A Cry for Love," at www.restorativejustice.org.

Chapter 4

Will Violence Bring Peace?

The myth of redemptive violence thrives whenever we assume that violence is an effective way to solve problems. Terrible as it is, we are tempted to believe that violence can bring good things out of a bad scene. Indeed, violence assumes a virtuous character whenever we expect it to save us from evil. The myth of redemptive violence fills video games, movies, and our usual interpretation of American history.

If we believe that violence works, that it redeems bad things, then we readily turn to it when we face aggression or exploitation. When we want to fix things that have gone awry, we reach for guns, bombs, and missiles. But sadly, when we try to redeem things through violent means, we may actually become the very evil we hate. A speaker at the national prayer service on September 14, 2001, urged us "not to become the evil we deplore."

Many of the writers in chapter 4 challenge the myth of redemptive violence. They dispute the belief that violent actions will bring a lasting, long-term peace. To fix bad things like terrorism, they suggest, we must search for its root causes and seek to address them. The writers contend that people of faith should abandon the myth of redemptive violence and instead seek to overcome evil with good.

A Hut of Shalom

Arthur Waskow

When the Jewish community celebrates the harvest festival, we build a "*sukkah,*" a fragile hut with a leafy roof. It's the most vulnerable of houses. Vulnerable in time because it only lasts a week each year. Vulnerable in space because its roof must be not only leafy but leaky—letting in starlight, and gusts of wind and rain.

In the evening prayers, we plead with God, "Spread over all of us Your Sukkah of shalom." Why a sukkah, a hut? Why does the prayer plead to God for a "sukkah of shalom" rather than God's tent or house or palace of peace?

Precisely because the sukkah is so vulnerable.

For much of our lives, we try to achieve peace and safety by building with steel and concrete and toughness: Pyramids, air-raid shelters, Pentagons, World Trade Centers. We harden what might be targets and, like Pharaoh, harden our hearts against what is foreign to us. But the sukkah comes to remind us: In truth, we all are vulnerable. If "a hard rain's a-gonna fall" (song by Bob Dylan), it will fall on all of us.

Americans have felt invulnerable. Our oceans, our wealth, and our military power have created what seemed to be an invulnerable shield. We may have begun feeling uncomfortable in the nuclear age, but no harm came to us. Yet yesterday the ancient truth came home: We all live in a sukkah.

Not only the targets but even the instruments of attack

were among our proudest possessions: sleek transcontinental airliners. They availed us nothing. Worse than nothing. Even the greatest oceans do not shield us. Even the mightiest buildings do not shield us. Even the wealthiest balance sheets and the most powerful weapons do not shield us.

There are only wispy walls and leaky roofs between us. The planet is in fact one interwoven web of life. The command to love my neighbor as I do myself is not an admonition to be nice: it is a statement of truth like the law of gravity (Lev. 19:8). For my neighbor and myself are interwoven. If I pour contempt upon my neighbor, hatred will recoil upon me.

What is the lesson of the sukkah? How do we make such a vulnerable house into a place of shalom, of peace and security and harmony and wholeness?

The lesson is that only a world where we all recognize our vulnerability can become a world where all communities feel responsible to all other communities. And only such a world can prevent such acts of rage and murder.

If I treat my neighbor's pain and grief as foreign, I will end up suffering when my neighbor's pain and grief curdle into rage.

But if I realize that the walls between us are full of holes, I can reach through them in compassion and connection.

The groups accused of this terror espouse a tortured version of Islam. Whether or not this turns out to be so, America must open its heart and mind to the pain and grief of those in the Arab and Muslim worlds who feel excluded, denied, unheard, disempowered, defeated.

This does not mean ignoring or forgiving whoever wrought such bloodiness. They must be found and brought to trial, without killing still more innocents and without wrecking still more the fragile sukkah of lawfulness. Their violence must be halted. But we must also reach beyond them—to calm the rage that gave them birth by addressing the pain from which they sprouted.

From festering pools of pain and rage sprout the plague of terrorism. Some people think we must choose between addressing the plague or addressing the pools that give it birth. But we can do both—if we focus our attention on these two distinct tasks.

To go to war against whole nations does neither. It will not apprehend the guilty for trial, and probably not even seriously damage their networks. It will not drain the pools of pain and rage; it is far more likely to add to them.

Instead of entering upon a "war of civilizations," we must pursue a planetary peace.

Rabbi Arthur Waskow is Director of the Shalom Center in Philadelphia and the author of Godwrestling Round 2. *Adapted from an essay (copyright 2001 by Arthur Waskow) on www.shalomwctr.org.*

Deny Them Their Victory

Religious Leaders Responding to Terrorism

We, American religious leaders, share the broken hearts of our fellow citizens. The worst terrorist attack in history that assaulted New York City, Washington (D.C.), and Pennsylvania has been felt in every American community.

Each life lost was of unique and sacred value in the eyes of God, and the connections Americans feel to those lives run very deep. In the face of such a cruel catastrophe, it is a time to look to God and to each other for the strength we need and the response we will make. We must dig deep to the roots of our faith for sustenance, solace, and wisdom.

First, we must find a word of consolation for the untold pain and suffering of our people. Our congregations will offer their practical and pastoral resources to bind up the wounds of the nation. We can become safe places to weep and secure places to begin rebuilding our shattered lives and communities. Our houses of worship should become public arenas for common prayer, community discussion, eventual healing, and forgiveness.

Second, we offer a word of sober restraint as our nation discerns what its response will be. We share the deep anger toward those who so callously and massively destroy innocent lives, no matter what the grievances or injustices invoked. In the name of God, we too demand that those responsible for these utterly evil acts be found and brought to justice. Those culpable must not escape accountability. But we must not, out of anger and vengeance, indiscriminately retaliate in ways that bring on even more loss of innocent life. We pray that President Bush and members of Congress will seek God's wisdom as they choose the appropriate response.

Third, we face deep and profound questions of what this attack on America will do to us as a nation. The terrorists have offered us a stark view of the world they would create, where the remedy to every human grievance and injustice is a resort to the random and cowardly violence of revenge—even against the most innocent. Having taken thousands of our lives, attacked our national symbols, forced our political leaders to flee their chambers of governance, disrupted our work and families, and struck fear into the hearts of our children, the terrorists must feel victorious.

But we can deny them their victory by refusing to submit to a world created in their image. Terrorism inflicts not only death and destruction but also emotional oppression to further its aims. We must not allow this terror to drive us away from being the people God has called us to be. We assert the vision of community, tolerance, compassion, justice, and the sacredness of human life, which lies at the heart of all our religious traditions. America must be a safe place for all our citizens in all their diversity. It is especially important that our citizens who share national origins, ethnicity, or religion with whoever attacked us are, themselves, protected among us.

Our American illusion of invulnerability has been shattered. From now on, we will look at the world in a different way, and this attack on our life as a nation will become a test of our national character. Let us make the right choices in this crisis—to pray, act, and unite against the bitter fruits of division, hatred, and violence. Let us rededicate ourselves to global peace, human dignity, and the eradication of injustice that breeds rage and vengeance.

As we gather in our houses of worship, let us begin a process of seeking the healing and grace of God.

This ecumenical statement was developed in consultation with Jewish, Muslim, and Christian clergy and signed by more than 3,900 religious leaders. The breadth of participation has made the document one of the most inclusive religious statements ever released. Reprinted with permission from Sojourners, *www.sojo.net. (Telephone 800-714-7474.)*

What Can We Do About Terrorism?

Robert M. Bowman

Mr. President, you did not tell the American people the truth about why we are the targets of terrorism. You said we are targets because we stand for democracy, freedom, and human rights in the world. Baloney!

We are the targets of terrorists because we stand for dictatorship, bondage, and human exploitation in the world. We are the targets of terrorists because we are hated. And we are hated because our government has done hateful things, such as deposing popularly elected leaders and replacing them with puppet military dictators willing to sell out their people to American multinational corporations. We are not hated because we practice democracy, freedom, and human rights, but because we deny these things to people in the developing nations.

In response to September 11, Steve Dunleavy of the *New York Post* screams, "Kill the bastards! Train assassins, hire mercenaries, put a couple of million bucks up for bounty hunters to get them dead or alive, preferably dead. As for cities or countries that host these worms, bomb them into basketball courts."

It's tempting to agree. I have no sympathy for the psychopaths who killed thousands of our people. There is no excuse for such acts. If I were recalled to active duty, I would go in a heartbeat.

Yet all my military experience and knowledge tells me that retaliation hasn't rid us of the problem in the past, and won't this time. By far the world's best anti-terrorist apparatus is Israel's. Measured in military terms, it has been phenomenally successful. Yet Israel still suffers more attacks than all other nations combined. If retaliation worked, Israelis would be the world's most secure people.

Only one thing has ever ended a terrorist campaign: denying the terrorist organization the support of the larger community it represents. And the only way to do that is to listen to and alleviate the legitimate grievances of the people. If Osama bin Laden was behind the four hijackings and subsequent carnage, that means addressing the concerns of Arabs and Muslims in general and of Palestinians in particular.

It does not mean abandoning Israel. But it may mean withdrawing financial and military support until they abandon the settlements in occupied territory and return to 1967 borders. It may also mean allowing Arab countries to have leaders of their own choosing, not hand-picked, CIA-installed dictators willing to cooperate with Western oil companies. Chester Gillings has said it well:

> How do we fight back against bin Laden?
>
> The first thing we must ask ourselves is, What do we hope to achieve: security or revenge? The two are mutually exclusive; seek revenge, and we will reduce our security. If it is security we seek, then we must begin to answer the tough questions: What are the grievances of the Palestinians and the Arab world against the United States? What is our real culpability for those grievances?
>
> Where we find legitimate culpability, we must be prepared to cure the grievance wherever possible. Where we cannot find culpability or a cure, we must communicate

honestly our positions directly to the Arab people. In short, our best course of action is to remove ourselves as a combatant in the disputes of the region.

To kill bin Laden now would make him an eternal martyr. Thousands would rise up to take his place. In another year, we would face another round of terrorism, probably much worse than this one. Yet there is another way. In the short term, we must protect ourselves from those who already hate us, by increased security and better intelligence.

In March 2001, I proposed to Congress that we should deny any funds for Star Wars until the Executive shows they are doing all possible research on detecting and intercepting weapons of mass destruction entering the country clandestinely—a far greater threat than ballistic missiles.

There are lots of steps that can be taken to increase security without detracting from civil rights. But in the long term, we must change our policies to stop causing the fear and hatred that creates new terrorists.

We need to become independent of foreign oil through conservation, energy efficiency, production of energy from renewable sources, and a transition to nonpolluting transportation. Such action will allow us to adopt a more rational policy toward the Middle East. The vast majority of Arabs and Muslims are good, peaceful people. But enough of them, in their desperation and anger and fear, have turned first to Arafat and now to bin Laden to relieve their misery.

Remove the desperation, give them some hope, and support for terrorism will evaporate. At that point, bin Laden will be forced to abandon terrorism (as has Arafat) or be treated like a common criminal. Either way, he and his money cease to be a threat. We can have security, or we can have revenge. We cannot have both.

Dr. Robert M. Bowman, *Lt. Col., USAF, retired, directed all the "Star Wars" programs under Presidents Ford and Carter and flew 101 combat missions in Vietnam. He is President of the Institute for Space and Security Studies and Presiding Archbishop of the United Catholic Church. Adapted from a letter to President Bush, published at www.rmbowman.com.*

Following Jesus in the Face of Terror

J. Denny Weaver

The events of September 11 shocked the world. Since then, we have witnessed an escalating, patriotic outcry about the need to "do something." President Bush has assured the world that he will do something. These events challenge the faithfulness of the church.

Revelation holds a precedent and an answer. Each of the seals in Revelation 6 uses symbols to refer to events during the reigns of first-century Roman emperors, such as Tiberius, under whose rule Jesus was killed, or Domitian, emperor when the book was written. The sixth seal corresponds to Emperor Vespasian, during whose reign a Roman army destroyed the sacred city of Jerusalem. The images of earthquake, celestial collapse, and panic in the streets in Revelation 6:12-17 all depict the destruction and accompanying feelings of loss and despair. Today Americans can empathize with what the residents of Jerusalem felt in 70.

Revelation 7:10-12 features a song of celebration for the victory of the reign of God. John shows that while the forces of evil appear to have a momentary victory, in the resurrection of Jesus, even the worst imaginable evil, the destruction of Jerusalem, is overcome. These words from Revelation apply today. In the face of overwhelming evil, our faith and hope rest in the resurrection of Jesus rather than in any earthly, political entity.

But we need to respond now, in this world. Here also our answer rests with Jesus Christ. To be Christian is to be Christlike, to live within the story of Jesus. The church's response to the events of September 11 should reflect the way of Jesus rather than simply mirror the violence of that day.

Many voices have asked the nation to do something. But what does "doing something" mean?

Do nothing or use violence. First, recognize the assumptions behind the push to doing something. It really means to do something violent. One assumption is that only two options exist: either do nothing or use violence. A second assumption is that if violence is used, it will succeed.

The people who committed these horrific deeds thought that violence would work. Every war and violent conflict proceeds on the assumption that violence works. But since each side believes violence works, violence is actually guaranteed to fail half the time. Since the "winning side" also experiences losses, outcomes are less than clear-cut. President Bush assured us that the coming war in Afghanistan will be protracted and difficult. As Christians following the way of Jesus encounter the patriotic rush to do something, they should remember that violence does not always work.

When each side believes that only violence will resolve a problem, each act of retaliation, to teach the other side a lesson, only provokes another cycle of violence. This cycle flows from the belief held by each side that violence is the only way to respond.

Other Options. Refusing to support military retaliation is not a call for inaction or a call for the church to withdraw. Our options are *not* limited to using violence or doing nothing. We must propose other options that do not nourish the cycle of violence. We need to ask what causes such hatred against the United States.

Is it relevant, for example, that the United States, with some 4 percent of the world's population, consumes about 40 percent of the world's resources? Does pulling that much of the world's resources into this country have anything to do with poverty in other countries? Yes, it creates resentment. Does this wealthy nation's support of the ongoing occupation of Palestinian territory contribute to the hostility the United States engenders in the world? I am sure it does.

Organizations such as Christian Peacemaker Teams (CPT) address these problems through witness activities that call attention to violence and injustice in hot spots around the world. Other church-related agencies address systemic injustice through programs of material and developmental aid and by educating North Americans about the realities of systemic violence.

Active peacemaking. The efforts of these agencies, however, are small in view of the church's potential and the violence in the world. We have barely begun to research techniques for active nonviolent peacemaking in national and international conflicts. We have committed few resources to active peacemaking in international contexts. CPT receives only token funding from sponsoring Mennonite, Brethren, and Quaker denominations. During World War II, the peace churches spent about $3 million on Civilian Public Service in seven years. In today's dollars, that would be around $23 million. Does the church today have enough faith in the nonviolent story of Jesus to commit that much money in the next seven years to develop nonviolent peacemaking strategies and train our young people in implementing them?

Responding to September 11 is not a simple choice between doing nothing and violent retaliation. Nonviolent responses that address the causes of the cycle of violence may not seem patriotic, and they will not be as flashy as the violent responses of the Pentagon. But in the long view, such efforts will contribute more to peace than military ventures.

Nonviolent strategies do work. Gene Sharp and other writers report how nonviolence has worked in many settings. But effectiveness is not the primary reason for advocating nonviolence.

Jesus' mission. The ultimate reason for the church to develop nonviolent peacemaking is that it is Christian, it is central to the story of Jesus Christ. We confess Jesus as "the way, and the truth, and the life" (John 14:6). We are his disciples. Jesus came to introduce the peaceable reign of God in our history. Our calling as his disciples is to do likewise.

The resurrection of Jesus established the reign of God. We participate in and witness to that victory over evil by living within the story of Jesus, the victorious Lamb. "They have conquered [the accuser] by the blood of the Lamb and by the word of their testimony" (Rev. 12.11). Our lived testimony makes visible today the peaceable reign of God triumphing over evil in the resurrection of Jesus. Nonviolent peacemaking is central to our calling as Christians.

May God grant us wisdom and courage to live in the resurrection of Jesus while facing the violence of September 11 and the violence sure to happen in the coming weeks.

*J. **Denny Weaver** teaches theology and ethics at Bluffton (Ohio) College. Adapted from a sermon, September 16, 2001.*

Destroying Terrorists Weakens Our Security

Ron Kraybill

In the view of bin Laden and many Muslims, a powerful, prosperous, and wicked adversary towers over the worldwide Islamic community—the United States. They see us as evil because our troops occupy holy territory, Saudi Arabia, and because we back Israel, which has thrown Muslims out of their homeland in Palestine. We back oppressive and corrupt Muslim leaders, we bomb Iraq, and we spread sexual immorality via the media all over the world. Bin Laden believes he must wage holy war against us in the name of God.

Bin Laden's goal is to radicalize the Muslim community and multiply the number of recruits. He knows that nothing outrages complacent people like being the targets of military attack, as September 11 united us. To succeed, he hopes we will direct massive force against Muslims. Some, in anger, will join the extremists, and many more will provide quiet support. Voices of moderation will go silent.

Our security requires that we deprive bin Laden of a significant military response abroad. Not because we want to be nice, but because we must be realistic about winning the long-term struggle. If we make our goal to destroy bin Laden and associates at any cost, we may win the battle, but we will surely lose the long-term war for our true security. Even if we kill bin Laden and all his colleagues, the dynamics we help create will live on.

More pivotal to the security of America than the life or death of bin Laden is the long-term goodwill of the Islamic masses of the world. If they conclude that America is the enemy, they will make us permanently unsafe, long after bin Laden is gone. If they recognize in us a generous and respectful friend, they will marginalize bin Laden, assist us in bringing him to book, and discourage his sympathizers.

Thus our first criterion for any action must not be, "Does this help us destroy bin Laden?" Instead, it must be, "Will this help us develop the broad base of goodwill and appreciation among Muslims that is necessary if we wish to keep extremists at the margins of their communities?" Imagine the goodwill we would reap if we directed the billions already spent on the war effort to improving the well-being of Muslims worldwide.

We must take measures to protect ourselves against terrorists at home. But we dare not indulge in the dangerous fantasy that we can aggressively eliminate extremists abroad, for this will simply multiply our enemies. Instead, we must find another way to limit them. After all, extremists reside in all communities at all times, yet few ever advance their cause beyond the margins of their own societies.

Specifically, to respond to this unprecedented outbreak of terrorism, we must make space for constructive processes in the region of Afghanistan as well as in the Muslim community worldwide. These options may not immediately yield us bin Laden or the Taliban, but we have rightly been cautioned that this will be a long and difficult struggle.

What would we lose if instead of bombing, we focused on winning the hearts and minds of the Afghani people and their neighbors? Suppose we bombarded Afghans with food, medicine, seeds, and traditional farming implements for a year or two while blockading the importation of weapons and related technology?

We could assist the millions of Afghani refugees to begin forming a sustainable government. Maybe Muslim governments elsewhere in the world, starting perhaps with the Pakistanis, would engage their hard-line Taliban brothers in serious heart-to-heart talks. The UN might play a role. And given enough time, bin Laden would surface somewhere, betrayed perhaps by someone eager to assist his departure.

Could it work? No guarantees. But even partial success would bring us greater long-term security than a military rout of the Taliban that ignores Muslim perceptions worldwide. With weapons of mass destruction growing ever smaller and cheaper, we cannot be more than a generation or two from a time when a small number of persons will be able to create or acquire the means to destroy millions. The only thing worse than one bin Laden would be a dozen, a thousand, or a hundred thousand of him. To the extent that our actions confirm Muslim perceptions of us, we assist the creation of such a nightmare.

Ron Kraybill *is a Professor in the Conflict Transformation Program of Eastern Mennonite University (Harrisonburg, Va.). Adapted from an essay distributed on November 9, 2001, at www.emu.edu.*

False Gods Can't Save Us

Ron Adams

Like the world around us, we can, in our feelings of despair and confusion, eagerly take things into our own hands. We can decide it's up to us to bring justice, to repair the damage, to make things right. And we can use the tools at hand—guns, bombs, missiles, jets—to try to wipe the slate clean. But we might as well call on Baal to save us. The result of such efforts will be more death, more destruction, and more suffering. Destroying every terrorist, bombing every stronghold, burning every city in Afghanistan—all this will not bring one victim back to life. That power is simply not ours. We do not have the power to give life.

Many biblical stories offer an alternative voice to the ones calling us to take up arms against our enemies. They remind us that, even though false gods will always claim to give life, no one has the power to give life but God. To trust in anything or anyone else is simply idolatry.

These stories also remind us that God uses that life-giving power to bless every person on earth, even those we consider enemies. We cannot assume, as did the religious authorities of Jesus' day, that we are the only children of God, the only blessed ones, the only ones who can claim to be good. God does not honor such boundaries, such definitions, and such attempts to restrict and manipulate God's Spirit in the world.

The Bible calls us away from the racism and hatred that war-making has always required. It calls us to humility and wonder at a God who remains so much more than we can imagine. It encourages us to call upon God, praying that peace and justice will be extended to all, victims and perpetrators alike.

Ron Adams *pastors the East Chestnut Street Mennonite Church, Lancaster, Pennsylvania. Adapted from a sermon, September 16, 2001.*

Three Views of the Church and War

A. James Reimer

On the morning of September 11, I was driving to Toronto to teach my first class of the term. I heard on the radio that a plane hit the World Trade Center. When I arrived at the Toronto School of Theology, I watched as the Twin Towers collapsed. At 11 a.m. I began teaching my class on "War and Peace in Christian Thought." It explores different ways in which Christians throughout the ages have struggled with war and violence. The events of the day filled the class with a new sense of urgency and relevance.

Throughout history, rulers have defended their political interests and goals by using religious language. This is called propaganda. In the United States, president after president has called on religious leaders to sanction their personal moral life and their political actions. George W. Bush has done the same, using religious phrases like "Infinite Justice" and "The War Against Evil" to describe complex matters. Most religious believers have naively fallen in line with their rulers and interpreted their sacred texts to support the national self-interest. Christianity is no better, even though its founder taught the opposite and was crucified for it.

Consider a brief historical account of Christianity's rather blotchy record on this score. There have been three basic Christian understandings of war. First, a *crusade* or *holy war,* war fought in obedience to God's command. Second, the *just* or *justified war,* war recognized as wrong but necessary under certain circumstances. The just war can only be fought under strict conditions. Third, *pacifism*, the principled rejection of all bloodshed in obedience to Jesus' teachings of nonresistant love.

All three views can be supported by biblical texts (both Old and New Testaments). The crusade or holy war has been supported by texts like Exodus 15, where God is described as a holy warrior, or Revelation, where we read about the righteous war (cf. 13:7; 19:11).

The just war, fought according to strict rules, can be supported by Deuteronomy 20, where the Jews are told how to conduct themselves when they go to war. It also finds support in Romans 13: Paul says that all governments are ordained by God to bear the sword in order to restrain evil and protect the good, and that Christians are expected to obey their government.

A pacifist ethic can be supported with Old Testament texts like Isaiah 53, where the Messiah is described as a suffering servant, or by New Testament texts such as the Sermon on the Mount (Matt. 5). Most important, the life, teachings, and death of Jesus demonstrate Christian pacifism.

In the church's first two hundred years, its official teachings urged Christians not to join the military, though a few might have done so. Texts from near the end of the second century tell of Christian militia protecting bishops.

The church's view underwent a dramatic change in the period around A.D. 312, when Emperor Constantine became a Christian. Christians were no longer a persecuted minority but gradually became a privileged minority and then a majority. Earlier, *Christians* were not allowed in the Roman army; now, *non-Christians* were not allowed in the army.

In the fourth and fifth centuries, the just-war tradition developed. Christian theologians argued that war could only be fought when (a) a legitimate ruler proclaimed it, (b) the war's purpose was just—to restore peace, (c) the motivation was just—done with love of enemy and not as an act of vengeance, (d) innocent people were not killed, and so on.

Later just-war rules stipulated (e) for self-defense only, (f) exemption of priests, (g) proportionality—the harm done could not exceed the harm to be rectified, (h) certainty of victory, and so on.

Christians no longer based their ethical beliefs strictly on revelation and the teachings of Jesus but on human reasoning, on what makes sense. Most assumed that it does not make sense to expect the ruler to conduct his imperial responsibilities according to the Sermon on the Mount.

Some Christians continued to practice Jesus' pacifist ethic. Monastics headed for the desert, to live "without spot and blemish" (2 Pet. 3:14). However, even these monks and nuns could not always escape the snares of the devil and temptations of the flesh. Yet they tried to continue the vision of the earliest Christians.

In the high Middle Ages, the just-war tradition gave way to the crusade and the holy war. Religious leaders urged the faithful to go to Jerusalem and Constantinople, to liberate the holy sites from the infidels (Turks or Muslims). During the Crusades (centuries 11-13), Christians were much *less* tolerant of Muslim believers than Muslims were of Christians. Christians committed barbaric atrocities against Muslims. One exception was Francis of Assisi, who went to a Muslim caliph (supreme ruler of Islamic state) and tried to mediate between warring factions.

During the sixteenth-century Reformation, all three approaches to war (holy war, just war, and pacifism) were represented by various groups: Catholics, Lutheran, Reformed, Church of England, and Anabaptists. The Thirty Years' War (1618-48), one of the bloodiest in history, was driven by religious differences between the various Reformation groups. It was a time of incredible religious and political intolerance, religious dogmatism, and barbarism.

The eighteenth-century Enlightenment, sometimes described as the Age of Reason or Secularization, was a reaction and revulsion against religious bigotry and inhumanity. The birth of modernity (freedom, individualism, humanism, reaction against religion) was really a rejection of religions' historical alliance with the powers of oppression and domination.

The eighteenth and nineteenth centuries produced great hope and optimism. Secular pacifist movements were convinced that the world could be made better without the help of religion. Religion always seemed to be anti-human. But this modern, liberal view of progress collapsed with the wars and atrocities of the twentieth century, probably the most barbaric of all time.

Anabaptists have all three types in the family tree: Those seeing themselves as holy warriors, like Jan Matthys and Jan van Leyden, who took over the city of Münster, hoping to bring in the kingdom of God. Just-war types, like Balthasar

Hubmaier in Moravia. And those, like Conrad Grebel, who rejected violence, including that of the crusaders. After initial diversity, many of the Anabaptist groups came to emphasize pacifism, which has mostly continued up to the present.

Let me conclude with several reflections about how we might live creatively in a world of violence. I call on both Christians and Muslims not to be self-righteous in their own tradition. Neither of us always lives up to our sacred texts and teachings. Let us engage in a great jihad, the struggle to purify ourselves from evil. This is the primary Christian "War Against Evil."

We may be tempted to retreat as individuals or communities into the desert. Some may be called to do this, and we should be thankful for their example. But on the whole, we no longer have that option. At a time like this, our voice needs to be heard, calling for an "Infinite Justice" of another kind—eternal self-giving love for all peoples of whatever religion, race, or nation; a love that transcends our own North American interests.

Another temptation is to spout easy and often hypocritical answers, too easily using the religious jargon of peace and nonviolence. We live in a fallen world of sin, a world of evil and violence, where no perfect choices are available. What does it mean to live in such a world? Jesus said, "Render to Caesar the things that are Caesar's, and to God the things that are God's" (Mark 12:17, KJV).

Acts tells us of Paul's encounter with Jewish and Roman authorities. Peter and Paul face the wrath of the religious leaders for their preaching and then also experience Roman justice. Again and again, Paul claims his rights as a Roman citizen, accepts the military protection provided by the Roman rulers and their soldiers, and appeals to the emperor. Before

Paul was (likely) martyred in Rome, he struggled for justice in the highest courts of the land (Acts 21–28).

May God grant us grace to be wise as hawks and harmless as doves.

A. James Reimer is Professor of Religion and Theology at Conrad Grebel College/University of Waterloo and Toronto School of Theology. Adapted from a sermon, October 21, 2001.

From Just War to Holy War

Robert J. Suderman

The events of September 11 pose new questions about war. Indeed, the Christian faith is being used to justify a military response to the terrorist attacks. The language of U.S. leaders creates the impression that this is a holy war rather than a traditional just war. Just-war categories invite potential participants in war to consider whether or not a war is justified, according to well-established ethical criteria.

In a holy war, these criteria are ignored because they are not important. What is important in a holy war is that God declares it, not to restrain the enemy but to eradicate evil. Because it is God-initiated, human criteria play no part.

President Bush's response to September 11 borders on holy-war thinking. It is clothed in religious, biblical, and "Christian" rhetoric. The military objective is to rid the world of "evil," a statement that is not only unrealistic but also heretical.

People are to be brought dead or alive to justice. Options are narrowed. If you are not for us, then you are for the terrorists. If others pose alternatives, it puts them on the side of terrorists.

For Christians, who believe sin and evil must be dealt with in the context of God's redemptive work in Christ, the idea that the U.S. military can rid the world of evil is an affront to our faith. The shift from just-war status to holy war appeals to the undiscerning religious soul of America.

In the public "Christian" rhetoric, there is little of Christian insight and doctrine. Yes, God is often mentioned. The Bible is frequently quoted. Prayer is encouraged. Religious principles are affirmed.

But the cross and resurrection, the "twin towers" of Christian faith, are invisible. I have heard no one speak about the potential impact of the resurrection or the cross on projected public policy and the ethics of retaliation. I have heard no mention of forgiveness as the way we view the world and understand God.

Talk about compassion and love has been replaced by preconceptions of justice. Justice is something that is "done," either by bringing the enemy to it or taking it to the enemy. Justice is not something that is lived daily (and historically), which, if done, would make it a viable hope for the future.

We hear a lot of religious language, but the message is not Christian. Christian language and symbols are used, but the military responses are not Christian. These religious words and symbols create the impression of a holy war.

Robert J. Suderman *is Executive Secretary for the Christian Witness Council of the Mennonite Church Canada. Adapted from a* Mennonite Weekly Review *essay, October 4, 2001.*

Fighting Terrorism at Home?

Tamara Dorcel Lewis

The day after the tragedy, I listened to our first African-American Secretary of State, Colin Powell, declare war on terrorism. He vowed to rip apart terrorist cells and infiltrate network after network until terrorism was eradicated from our world. I also heard President Bush repeat Powell's pledge to rid the world of these "evildoers."

The events of September 11 have shaken a mighty nation and angered many who wish to punish those responsible for committing such shocking and hateful acts. As a patriotic American, I feel the same way. Indeed, hate is evil. In its most extreme form, hate terrorizes people whose only fault is embodying the image of scorn, belonging to a group identified by the terrorists as having no value.

I speak from experience, both past and present. And I fear living this nightmare, even as the United States moves to rid the world of the terrorists who indelibly rattled our confidence. You see, I'm an African-American, and there are people in my own country who will always hate me, devalue me, and fail to respect me. Some will label me unpatriotic for talking about such a divisive issue in times such as these. I love this country with all my heart. I love the ideals this country was built on, and I strive to make those ideals stand true for all. That, I believe, is the American way.

But I hurt because I am so confused. I have spent my adult

life teaching my sons to identify the overt and subtle signs of racism in those who hate them here in America, just because they are black. African-Americans accept these obstacles as a way of life. We realize that we can be successful and achieve our dreams. But we must be aware of the prejudicial road-blocks and draw on our resourceful nature if we are to attain our goals.

If we rid the world of these terrorists tomorrow, most Americans will be able to return to their lives, a bit shaken, but free from the terror I live with every day. It scares me that my children and I are not welcome in all American communities because we are black, or that white supremacist terrorists not only hate us but also have the means to harm us. In recent years, black churches have been burned down. An African-American man was dragged behind a truck until he was decapitated. Businesses have been found culpable in class-action discrimination suits because they denied African-Americans the same promotion opportunities as equally qualified whites.

As an African-American, I live with a legacy of hate that was born in slavery and has thrived, even as we have given our lives defending America from the Revolutionary War to the Gulf War. Yet our leaders are so insensitive to the pain that hate has caused in past and present that they refuse to recognize the history of slavery in the United States as the crime against humanity it represented then and represents now. Our pain is so insignificant to our leaders that they did not feel it necessary to attend the recent international conference on racism in South Africa.

Now, in the midst of the current tragedy, some Americans have resorted to killing and injuring people of Muslim faith and Arabic descent. I, again, fear for my life and the life of my family because our complexions could easily be mistaken as Middle Eastern. Are people using our current crisis as an excuse to attack dark-skinned people? Can you understand my confusion? Can you see that being the object of hate and racism is a way of life for me?

On a recent news program, experts reported that today's terrorists are different from those of the past. Today's terrorist can live among us, work with us, show no signs of obvious hate, but yet strike out at us, terrorize and alter our life and the lives of those we love and cherish.

As an African-American, that type of person does not surprise me. I have lived with that reality my whole life. Why are we still living with this after so many centuries? Why, as an American, do I have to warn children against domestic terrorists roaming the streets, causing physical, emotional, and economic harm to others simply because of religious views or color?

I pledge my allegiance to America and will dutifully fight for her freedom and the freedom of all citizens. But who will fight for me here at home? Who will turn to the neighbor and say that hate is wrong regardless of whether it is practiced by foreign terrorists or the man down the street? That those who bombed the World Trade Center and the Pentagon are no better or worse than those who bomb black churches and burn crosses on the lawns of black families? That those who attempt to disrupt the lives of Americans are no better than those who attempt to deny black families the right to live in any community in America? Hate is hate, no matter how you look at it and no matter where it comes from.

Those who espouse hate in our country are no different from the Taliban in Afghanistan. They are terrorists! Our government should work as hard to identify and eradicate domestic terrorism in all its forms, right here at home. They operate in political, military, and civilian networks that oppose the advancement of people they hate, devalue, and disrespect, people like me who represent a minority race.

Americans are asking, "Why do the foreign terrorists hate us so?" I ask the same question about our domestic terrorists. I can't seem to find an answer. When President Bush declared war on all "evildoers," I wondered if he was including domestic ones as well. Why don't all Americans do something about our own domestic evildoers? We know who they are, we know what they believe, we even know some of the crimes they've committed. Why are they free to roam these "free" United States? How can we stand up and tell the world that we are against terrorism, evil, and hate when we stand by and do nothing about the evildoers we have at home?

Tamara Dorcel Lewis is a freelance writer in Springfield, Virginia. Adapted from an article at www.Africana.com, September 27, 2001.

Chapter 5

Voices from Our Global Family

In the wake of September 11, some Muslims have talked about the "Nation of Islam," the Islamic family of faith that stretches across many countries. In a similar fashion, Christians often speak of "the body of Christ," the church, which likewise reaches around the world.

The global nature of the body of Christ also means that when one part of the body suffers, the whole body suffers (1 Cor. 12:26). Most of the entries in chapter 5 are letters from Christians in other countries, offering their prayers and condolences in the aftermath of September 11. Many of these believers are familiar with terror and suffering, and they offer counsel and wisdom. As brothers and sisters in our larger family, they too yearn for a stable global order anchored in peace and justice.

The global nature of the church complicates the involvement of Christians in international conflicts. Pledging allegiance to different countries in time of war, they may find themselves killing each other. Someone has proposed that warfare might wane if, as a first small step, the Christians of the world promised never to kill each other.

A Letter from Honduras

Claudia Patricia Carcamo

Do not let the darkness invade your life. Do not let bitterness soil your soul. Do not let hate fill your heart. Do not let desperation seize your mind. We will not let dividing lines, made by people, destroy humanity. We will not let race, language, religion, and geographic boundaries distance us from the people who need our love and understanding. People like those who attacked the United States on September 11, 2001.

From this day onward, we need three words, which will be more than words, if we practice them:

Humility, to recognize that there is forgiveness. That only by *not* responding with attacks do we show that we have not been overcome.

Pride, to walk with head held high, as human beings in solidarity and respect, raising up the country without harming innocent people.

Faith, to believe in God, more than in earthly life.

Claudia Patricia Carcamo, age 17, writing from Honduras to the people of the United States on the day of the attack.

A Letter from Guatemala

Latin American Anabaptist Seminary

Dear brothers and sisters in our shared walk to follow Jesus:

As believers in a God of Love and Peace that is present in all of history, we share with you our own experience. Many of us here in Guatemala and throughout Latin America have mourned the loss of loved ones, separated from life and from love by the selfish belligerence of others who believe that solutions can come through destruction and death. Our experiences of great bloodletting and war throughout Central America have persuaded us that there is no cause, religious or political, that warrants the loss of even one human life.

We have survived such desperation and fear because of our certainty that our Lord, creator of life, stands with the smallest, those who humbly place all of their trust in him. We believe that he has overcome death through the love of his risen Son. At the same time, we wish to share that our experience has taught us that God is among us today, washing away our tears with the noble acts of solidarity.

Perhaps the most significant signs of God's presence come in the everyday deeds of love for us from our neighbors, or even from the stranger who, in offering a hand, becomes the hand of God that wipes away our pain with our tears. Isaiah 25:8 says, "He will swallow up death forever. The Lord God will wipe away all tears and take away forever all insults and mockery against his land and people."

Teachers, students, and staff of the Latin American Anabaptist Seminary (Semilla) in Guatemala. Adapted from a letter.

A Letter from Colombia

Ricardo Esquivia Ballestas

Brothers and Sisters, may the peace of Jesus Christ guide you, accompany you, and comfort you.

Through the apostle Paul we know that in these end times, faced with violence and injustice, creation is crying out with birthing pain (Rom. 8:22-23). We, the global family of faith, groan with it, waiting for redemption. Brothers and sisters, every birth is painful. Through these acts that we suffer, God is inviting us to be birth parents of the new history where evil is overcome by good, where the enemy is loved, where we can all live without fear, and where nations respect the human dignity of all people on Earth.

The solidarity you have always showed for the pain of other peoples must not be lost with these recent acts of September 11. Rather, may your compassion increase with your own suffering and permit you to understand that it is in your country that the birthing process must begin. The United States is the center of the world, and what is done there has repercussions in the other countries of the world. Citizens of the United States, like all other peoples, will enjoy or suffer the consequences sooner or later. "Those who sow righteousness get a true reward" (Prov. 11:18).

We are filled with hope that you, from the center of the world, will begin a great campaign to keep the effects of evil, of hate, and of revenge from nesting in the souls of leaders and governments of the countries of the West. May you impede them from using their economic and military might against people of the East and of the Third World who are as innocent as the inhabitants of New York and Washington. They were victims of humans alienated by pain, hate, and hunger for vengeance.

Let us unite in a great campaign of fasting, prayer, preaching, and song. Thus we can rise to the challenge of taking to your leaders, the government of the United States, and to governments West and East, the message that violence only brings more violence, that "hate is like salt water; the more one drinks, the thirstier one gets."

It is time for the peoples of the earth to treat one another with respect, dignity, and solidarity. Only then can they calm the thirst of hate and vengeance felt by people who have been historically mistreated. War will only produce more hate and vengeance, and the people of the United States will only live in permanent anxiety.

It is time to birth a new world order, and the United States has the opportunity to show the rest of the world how to live with justice, without violence, without acts of death and destruction of innocent human lives. Teach us how to return good for evil and thus take away from the terrorists the excuse for a holy war of hate and death.

Your brother in Christ and humanity.

Ricardo Esquivia Ballestas directs the Commission of Human Rights and Peace of the Council of Evangelical Churches of Colombia. Adapted from a letter translated by Janna Bowman.

Boomerang Violence
A Dangerous Game

Janna Bowman and Bonnie Klassen

Colombians too are shaken by the monstrous tragedy of September 11. They grieve for the horrible violation of human life. These sisters and brothers understand the pain of death and destruction, for they have suffered a lifetime of loss. They endure the effects of deep-seeded hatred and vengeance in their land. They weep for the magnitude of the loss, showing humanity's distance from Christ's principles of justice and peace, and weep out of concern for vengeance. The global family is learning that when one member suffers, the whole body suffers (1 Cor. 12:26).

There is no moral, religious, or strategic justification for the calculated murder of thousands. However, our experience here shows that people who live with a feeling of structural injustice eventually attack the structure. Without forcing logic onto evil, lessons can be found in the rubble.

Those of us from the United States can ask ourselves, "Why were people in diverse countries smug with the symbolism in the attack on the World Trade Center towers and the Pentagon? What is it about U.S. lifestyles, the nation's global relationships, and its policies that lead people to sympathize with such violence?"

The acts of September 11 can be seen as symptoms of the cycles of revenge and violence used to redress injustices by the powerful, who have a stranglehold on our world. The injustice and war we've exported have come home.

In the Colombian context, the government reacted with a military response when desperate people resorted to violent means for seeking change. Rather than addressing the profound injustices of exclusion and poverty, which lead peasants to turn to despair and take up arms, the state strengthened its security forces, and the wealthy elites created self-defense groups.

Fifty years and over 150,000 violent deaths later, the war rages on. The fundamental issues here remain unresolved. The conflict only grows in complexity, with multinational business investments, and weapons and military training from the United States. Military solutions only intensify the cycle of violence, sucking in more actors, leading to greater insecurity for more people, and causing more destruction. The lessons from Colombia show the inadequacy of retaliatory measures in response to violent attacks.

The faith community must proclaim the message that "violence only brings more violence." Ignoring the root causes of resentment and hatred resolves nothing. Vengeful violence does not kill the motivation to rebel against oppressive powers.

People of faith can model loving, just relationships across national boundaries. We can be a testimony to peace and trusting relationships, challenging governments that seek security in military defense and revenge (cf. Eph. 3:10). Sustainable solutions are found in collective efforts to heal a broken world, not in lashing out against the perpetrator. Injustice and violence are problems belonging to all of us. Their solutions depend on our cooperation with one another and on our faith in a God who craves for peace.

Janna Bowman and Bonnie Klassen are involved with the Sanctuary Sister Church Commission in Colombia.

A Letter from Burkina Faso

Hulene Montgomery and Michael Graham

Dear Friends in America:

Throughout this day friends of yours in Burkina Faso have visited to search for news of your safety and to pray for peace. People are shocked and fearful of what this means. They are profoundly saddened by this violence. Last night Ousmane said, "All of Burkina is crying." Rasmani rushed into our home to embrace us and share his deep sympathy. Friends from the Language School called in shock. Pastor Samuel Yameogo prayed with us for the victims. Fidele and Jeanne Lompo dropped by this evening to pray for all the families and for peace between Christians and Muslims in Jos and throughout the world.

There have been so many others who have also called or visited to share their shock and deep sympathy. Many are afraid of what this means for world relations. Many have said that more violence is not the response. Many spoke of the need to stop the globalization agenda, which has left a few with so much and so many with so little. And people are concerned that this not lead to further tensions between Muslims and Christians.

May God comfort you and give you peace.

Hulene Montgomery and Michael Graham live in Burkina Faso.

A Letter from South Africa

Peter Storey

Dear Friends in the United States:

We mourn with you. Because we know and love so many of you, and have lived long enough among you to feel at least a measure of your hurt.

We continue to spend most of our days watching the layers of pain unfold across your land. From time to time, my mind closes down from overload, unable to hold the measure of horror.

We have been moved, as always, by the response of so many, acting so rapidly, and with purpose, to bring succor, ministering to the nation's wounds. There is something deeply stirring about the capacity of the American people to mobilize communities for good.

In the service at the National Cathedral, however, the church did not help President Bush, nor did it further the gospel. It was sad to see the church (and other religious traditions) laid so supinely at the disposal of Caesar and his chaplains. It is one thing for the church to invite the leaders of the land to come like any others, to pray, to seek God's healing and the guidance of God's word. It is theologically an entirely different matter to provide a pulpit to the head of state, enabling him to use a house of worship to rally the nation for war, exactly contradicting some of the Scriptures that were read.

When uniforms and flags crowd God's house, it is hard for God's word to be heard. Did it occur to anyone just how much this action resembled the way political leaders of some extreme Muslim fundamentalist states use their mosque pulpits for political purposes?

After that carefully choreographed exercise, faithful preachers will not have an easy task. As my preacher son said, "It will be difficult to balance the personal and pastoral on one hand, and the political or prophetic on the other."

Yet, as always, both dimensions exist in this atrocity. To weep with Jesus over the city's wounds is our pastoral imperative. To do so without asking his deep questions about why we do not recognize "the things that make for peace," is a dereliction of our calling (Luke 19:42).

In the midst of the weeping for the pain, which has given way so rapidly to cries for vengeance, should we not listen for another note—that of repentance? Some questions leap out at me. How is it that we continue to be defrauded by the false security of military might? The greatest military power on earth has been struck at its heart by three of its own commercial airliners, held to ransom by a handful of knife-wielding fanatics.

Yet nothing in the rhythm of human stupidity is likely to change. The saber-rattling will grow louder, the outworn weapons of war will be dusted off, and soon, somewhere in the "third world," the world I live in—many more people will die, adding to God's tears.

More hatred will be stored up in the ruins of some dusty country. We must bear witness to another way—the Jesus way of nonviolence. This is never more difficult than when we feel our loved ones and ourselves to be under attack, yet that is the time when such a witness is supremely relevant.

When will we have the courage to identify all fundamentalism as the well from which hatred drinks? Fundamentalism—Christian, Muslim, Hindu, Jewish, whatever—is surely the enemy of each of these faiths and will continue to turn them into instruments of division and death instead of life.

It is right to ask in horror, "What kind of people can perform such hateful, deranged deeds?" But there is also another question: "What have we done that leads to anybody hating us so much?" This is a hard question to ask at a time of such pain, but we pray that out of all this horror, there may be a better capacity to hear it (though I fear the opposite).

Part of the response to that question may be simply that the big boy on the block is always disliked by all the little guys who wish they were as big. But it's not as simple as that. There is a myth, cherished by the vast majority of Americans, that their nation's foreign and economic policy is both moral and benign. Yet from other vantage points it is viewed very differently.

I have often suggested to American Christians that the only way to understand their mission is to ask what it might have meant to witness faithfully to Jesus in the heart of the Roman Empire. Certainly, when I preach in the United States, I feel as I imagine the apostle Paul felt when he first passed through the gates of Rome—admiration for its people, awe at its manifest virtues, and resentment of its careless power.

American preachers have a task more difficult, perhaps, than those faced by us under South Africa's apartheid, or Christians under Communism. We had obvious evils to engage; you have to unwrap your Christian faith from the mythology of red, white, and blue.

You have to expose and confront the great *disconnect* between, on one hand, the kindness, compassion, and caring of most American people, and on the other, the ruthless way

American power is experienced, directly and indirectly, by the poor of the earth. You have to help good people see how they have let their institutions do their sinning for them. This is not easy among people who really believe that their country does nothing but good. But it is necessary, not only for their future, but for us all.

All around the world are those who believe in the basic goodness of the American people, who agonize with you in your pain, but also long to see your human goodness translated into a different, more compassionate way of relating with the rest of this bleeding planet.

With love and solidarity.

Rev. Dr. Peter Storey, former Methodist Bishop of the Johannesburg/Soweto area in South Africa, is now on the faculty of Duke Divinity School. He was on leave for fall 2001 in his native South Africa. Adapted from a letter he wrote on September 13, 2001.

A Letter from the Congo

Mesach Krisetya and Larry Miller

Dear Sisters and Brothers:

From the moment of the first news of the tragic events of September 11 and during the difficult weeks since then, the worldwide family of faith has been holding you up in heartfelt prayer. We traveled through restricted areas in the Congo, where Mennonites and their compatriots have been suffering under the effects of war, economic collapse, political crisis, and more than two million deaths. Expressions of grief and solidarity with Americans and with you in particular are prominent in nearly every meeting and worship service. Those we meet ask us to assure you of their fraternal love and fervent prayers.

These same sisters and brothers also ask if you are keeping your eyes fixed on Jesus Christ (Luke 4:20; Heb. 12:2). From their own life situation, they know you now face heavy pressure and high obstacles as you seek to follow and bear witness to the Savior, who loves enemies. They believe a warlike response to the September 11 violence will harm many people and impede Christian witness around the world, directly or indirectly, including here in Africa.

They encourage you to seek a message from God amid the present events and seize this opportunity to reinforce your proclamation of the gospel of peace, as they have tried to do during the war years in the Congo.

May God give you the strength to "run with perseverance the race marked out for [you]" (cf. Heb. 12:1, NIV).

Keep the faith!

Mesach Krisetya, President of Mennonite World Conference, lives in Indonesia. Larry Miller, Executive Secretary of Mennonite World Conference, lives in France. Adapted from a letter written from the Congo, October 7, 2001.

A Letter from Sri Lanka

Vinoth Ramachandra

The suicide attacks in the United States were acts of indescribable evil. All decent men and women everywhere should feel a deep sense of moral outrage. Jesus, the icon of God, showed anger when faced with human hard-heartedness and religious indifference to suffering. But that same Jesus refused to fight evil with evil, and challenged his disciples to overcome evil with good. If we treat others the way they treat us, or only show compassion and anger when our friends and family suffer, how are we different from others? (Luke 6:27-36). That was, and remains, the challenge of Christian discipleship, for which the Holy Spirit empowers us.

Christians seek justice, not revenge. Justice in a situation such as this has to do with collecting, weighing, and presenting evidence; respecting the rule of international law; and not being disproportionate or arbitrary in punishment. Even the much-maligned Old Testament principle of an "eye for eye" was never a prescription for blanket retaliation (Exod. 21:24). In a legal context, it sets limits to what punishment could be meted out to an individual. (If I took out your eye in a fight, the court should not take my life).

America has constantly obstructed all global efforts to set up an international criminal court, to try those accused of crimes against humanity. Ironically, both the United States and Afghanistan have appeared in the eyes of the world over the past year as "rogue states," nations that want to go it alone on the world stage, to refuse to submit to the claims of the international community.

What lessons can we learn from this horrendous tragedy?

We suffer together. What happens in other peoples' backyards eventually affects our own homes and families. In our globally interconnected world, we know that commodity or foreign-exchange speculations on Wall Street can cripple, say, an African nation's entire economy. Now we know that what happens in a Palestinian refugee camp can cripple Wall Street. We can no longer turn our backs on the hurts and brokenness of peoples living on the other side of the world.

History is important. These events didn't arise in a vacuum. They are the latest links in a tragic chain of numerous acts of brutality, cowardice, and broken promises that have marred the Middle East since the colonial breakup of the Ottoman Empire and the Balfour Declaration of 1917. Americans need to take the trouble to investigate, to learn about the peoples whose histories have suddenly enmeshed with your own. Many of the petty, despotic regimes of the Middle Eastern and Gulf states have been propped up by American and British governments and companies.

There are no safe havens in this world. Many from Asia, Africa, and Latin America flock to the United States in search of personal and economic "security." The economic might of USA (symbolized by the twin towers of the World Trade Center), all its military might (symbolized by the Pentagon), and all the think tanks and the billions of dollars poured into intelligence-gathering technology—all these things did not save America from this tragedy. And they never will.

Remember that most Christians in the world live outside Western nations. Christians in Pakistan, Indonesia, and other majority-Muslim countries fear the backlash from an indiscriminate air strike by the USA against Afghanistan. These are your brothers and sisters in Christ. We need to learn to think and respond not primarily as Americans, but as Christians who belong to a global community, the body of Christ, which claims our final allegiance.

The famous Barmen Declaration of 1934, produced by some Christian leaders in Germany to counter the subversion of the church by the Nazis, reminds us:

> All the churches of Jesus Christ, scattered in diverse cultures, have been redeemed for God by the blood of the Lamb to form one multicultural community of faith. The "blood" that binds them as brothers and sisters is more precious than the "blood," the language, the customs, political allegiances, or economic interests that may separate them. We reject the false doctrine, as though a church should place allegiance to the culture it inhabits and the nation to which it belongs above the commitment to brothers and sisters from other cultures and nations, servants of the one Jesus Christ, their common Lord, and members of God's new community.

Let the dreadful events of September 11, in the merciful providence of God, lead to a deeper humility among all of us—with Americans recognizing the limits of power and becoming willing to embrace weakness—and to a deeper commitment to pursue a more just and equitable world order. Then those Americans who died will not have died in vain.

Vinoth Ramachandra, *Colombo, Sri Lanka, is Regional Secretary for South Asia International Fellowship of Evangelical Students. This was adapted from a letter (www.urbana.org) written September 19, 2001.*

A Letter from Palestine

Ghassan Andoni

I cannot find the words to condemn and condole. What happened is beyond words. Make no mistake, the evil minds and the cold inhuman hearts that planned and executed this horrendous act of terror, can never be on the side of justice. They should not be allowed to shelter behind the suffering of my people. They have no respect for human lives. They should not be allowed to claim that they act on behalf of oppressed people. Such people are only loyal to their warlords. Nobody on the face of the earth can do more harm to Palestinians than this terror group did.

Yes, the American official policy causes us tremendous suffering. We have no doubt that without the blind backing of the U.S. government, Israel could not have gone this far in its terror campaign against Palestinians and could not impose this deep and unbearable level of injustice. Yet the innocent Americans inside the kidnapped airplanes and the thousands killed on the ground are not my enemy. Anyone who thinks differently can never belong to the same nation I belong to and believe deeply in its just cause.

We cannot fight for human rights using inhuman means. We can never be sensitive to human suffering if we think the lives of others are cheap. We can never struggle for justice and peace if we allow ourselves to use the inhuman means of occupiers and oppressors. We cannot allow a hundred years of imposed oppression and occupation to turn us into oppressors. I feel so ashamed of the few among us who even smiled while watching the drastic scene. I know for sure that the vast majority of Palestinians are shocked and sad, deeply sharing the pain of the victims and their families.

I want Americans to know, especially the ones we know and work with, that the vast majority of Palestinians are standing with you in these hard and dark times. We are ready to join hands with all interested, to be sure that such an ugly inhuman act will not happen again.

At the same time, I want to warn us all against the ones who are knocking the drums of war, who are playing to the hands of the ruthless terrorists—the ones who want this to turn into an open war between nations or religions. We need to work together to strip those inhuman groups from any popular support. This can only be done if our commitment for peace and justice overcomes our desire for revenge. This can only happen if our love and care for each other overcomes our hatred and anger.

We can never counter oppression and injustice with inhuman acts, or counter terrorism with acts of terror.

We pray for the families who grieve the loss of their dear ones. We ask God to provide them with the necessary strength to pass through these dark times. At the same time, we all have to work together for this not to happen again—not in the United States or anywhere else.

Finally, we confirm our commitment to intensify our work for peace and justice.

Ghassan Andoni directs the Palestinian Center for Rapprochement in Beit Sahour (near Bethlehem). Adapted from a letter.

Faces of Violence in Palestine/Israel

Alain Epp Weaver

"Is it true that Palestinians were celebrating in the streets?" my father asked me in a pained, worried tone over the phone. I had called my parents from my home in Jerusalem, where I direct a peace-building project, to reassure them of our safety after September 11.

The short answer to my father's question was yes. In the immediate aftermath of the attacks, small numbers of Palestinians did celebrate in East Jerusalem, Ramallah, and Nablus. But this short answer is *incomplete* and *misleading.*

Incomplete, because the vast majority of Palestinians were not celebrating. They were shocked, saddened, and horrified at these mass attacks on civilians. For at least a week after the attacks, the phones and fax machine at our office in East Jerusalem were tied up by Palestinian partners and friends sending condolences. Some broke down in tears as they spoke, and others were clearly as numb as I.

Palestinians gathered outside the U.S. Consulate on Nablus Road for a candlelight vigil of mourning and grief. Students in Palestinian schools observed a minute of silence. Palestinian Christian churches held prayer services for the victims. Many Palestinians here have relatives in the United States, and worried that family members would become victims of hate crimes in revenge for the attacks.

Misleading, because to focus on the few Palestinians who did celebrate (and were condemned in Palestinian society) serves to perpetuate the stereotype of the Palestinian as terrorist. Following September 11, the Israeli government has tried to equate all Palestinian resistance as terrorism and Palestinian leader Yassir Arafat with Osama bin Laden.

There should be no doubt that suicide bombings aimed at killing and terrorizing a civilian population are immoral. A simple condemnation of suicide bombings, however, presents only a small picture of reality in Israel and the occupied territories of the West Bank, East Jerusalem, and the Gaza Strip. For example, Palestinians with whom we work feel terrified of, and even terrorized by, the violence on which Israel's military occupation depends.

Over the past year, during the Palestinian Intifada (uprising) against Israel's military occupation, some 700 Palestinians have been killed. In the United States, that would be like 70,000 being killed. But weren't these Palestinian victims engaged in violent attacks against Israel—making them different from civilians at work in the World Trade Center or Israeli civilians at a disco in Tel Aviv?

Once again, reality proves complex. Of the 700 Palestinians killed, 60 percent died apart from confrontations with the Israeli military. Sixteen-year-old Johnny Yusef Taljieh, for example, was shot dead by an Israeli bullet while leaving mass at the Church of the Nativity in Bethlehem. Three-month-old Iman Hijo was killed in her mother's arms outside her family home in Khan Younis. Another 35 percent of these were killed during confrontations not involving firearms, for such things as stone-throwing.

Only 5 percent of the 700 dead of the past year were killed in armed clashes with the Israeli military. And most of these violent clashes were not suicide bombings but military actions within the occupied territories. International law does not prohibit an occupied people from resisting military occupation with violence. So should all such armed resistance be described as terrorism?

If terrorism is a disruption of one's everyday sense of security, then it is accurate to say that Israeli military occupation has terrorized millions of Palestinians. House demolitions, bombardments decried by international human rights organizations as excessive and disproportionate, soldiers at roadblocks who prevent people from reaching schools, hospitals, businesses, jobs, or homes at the point of a gun—all generate enormous insecurity among Palestinians.

As Christian pacifists, we condemn all forms of violence. We decry the ways in which myths of security built on violence, or liberation through violence, hold Israelis and Palestinians captive. Yet this blanket condemnation of violence cannot keep us from recognizing the different forms violence can take, and from questioning the moral value of labeling all violent resistance to a violent military occupation as "terrorism."

Prophetic voices within Israel are crying out that the occupation and its violence must end. Prophetic Palestinian voices proclaim that violent resistance to occupation—even when legitimate under international law—is militarily ineffectual, counterproductive, and not able to soften the hard heart of the occupiers. As the world prosecutes its war on terrorism, may we be steadfast in our solidarity with these prophets of Palestine/Israel who resist violence in all forms.

Alain Epp Weaver is Country Representative for Mennonite Central Committee in the occupied Palestinian territories.

War Harms Mission

Paul Schrag

Christians who support mission outreach among Muslims and approve of the U.S. war in Afghanistan support contradictory actions.

The war is at odds with sharing the gospel because much of the Muslim world perceives it as yet another clash between people of competing religions.

To citizens of the United States the war is "Americans Versus Terrorists." To many of the world's 1.2 billion followers of Islam, it is "Christians Versus Muslims."

It's rather clear that you can't share the love of Jesus with Muslims by dropping bombs on them.

Pacifist Christians have long pointed out that every war stands in conflict with the great commission (Matt. 28:18-20). The enemy soldier or civilian is either a Christian or not. If a Christian, how can one kill a fellow believer? If not a Christian, how can one send that person into eternity without a chance to hear of God's love? This is one of the reasons I believe a Christian must not kill.

In the current war, the contradiction between war and the Christian mission is magnified. This stems from the history of Christian-Muslim relations and from the way many Muslims perceive the unity of religion, culture, and government.

Much of the Islamic world thinks of Christianity as the religion that has made bloody incursions into Muslim lands.

Most painfully remembered are the Crusades, the European invasions to recapture the Holy Land from 1095 to 1272. To Westerners, these eight Crusades are ancient history. To Muslims, they remain a key part of defining Christianity as the aggressor and the enemy.

British and French colonial exploitation of the Arab world solidified this perception. Most recently, the Persian Gulf War reaffirmed this way of thinking.

Americans can rightly claim that the war in Afghanistan is not about religion. We can point out that the U.S. government does not represent the Christian church. But a great many Muslims outside the United States make little or no distinction between American actions and Christian actions. Islam places a great trust in political religion, and Muslims tend to view Christianity in similarly political terms.

Understanding these perceptions can help Christians see why the war in Afghanistan adds one more hindrance to the already difficult task of sharing the gospel in the Islamic world. Christians today must reclaim the gospel from its violent distortions. From the Crusades to the present, Muslims have seen plenty of evidence that Christianity is warlike and aggressive. They have seen far too few examples of its true nature as peaceful and loving.

"The words of Jesus about peacemaking, and the stories about his gentleness, go out into the Muslim world with great power," writes Gordon D. Nickel in *Peaceable Witness Among Muslims*. Nickel gives examples of the impact the gospel has made on Muslims who have known the friendship of Christians living in Jesus' peaceful way.

Today, U.S. warplanes, bombs, and soldiers are going out into the Muslim world with great power. Is it any wonder that the gospel of peace is virtually unknown there?

How might Jesus' message be received differently if Christians put their violent history behind them and vowed never to kill another Muslim?

Paul Schrag *is editor of* Mennonite Weekly Review. *From his November 1, 2001 editorial.*

Chapter 6

Citizens of Two Kingdoms

Christians carry two passports. They hold citizenship in the global kingdom of God as well as in a specific nation. How do they balance the duties of dual citizenship in the kingdom of God and in the kingdoms of this world?

Jesus told his followers, "Give to Caesar what is Caesar's and to God what is God's" (Mark 12:17, NIV). What exactly belongs to Caesar? To God? When does allegiance to country compete with allegiance to God? Should Christians fly the flag and sing "God Bless America"?

Many events flowing from September 11 were couched in religious words and symbols. Flag and cross merged together. Scriptures from the Koran and the Bible were quoted to justify war. Both Allah and God were asked to bless violence. The attackers appealed to Allah for blessing, and soon Americans were singing "God Bless America" as their nation prepared for war.

National leaders in both America and Afghanistan were speaking of evil, God, holy war, blessings, infidels, and Satan. Strands of patriotism, revenge, hate, prayer, and divine blessings were twisted into a single bundle of taut emotions.

The entries in chapter 6 explore these issues and ask how Christians can champion the religious freedom they enjoy in the United States without bowing to the altar of nationalism.

American Versus Heavenly Citizenship

David E. Nisly

I thank God that I am an American citizen and privileged to live in this country. Since September 11, patriotism has become a symbol of America's unity against the perpetrators of this evil. In the D.C. area, thousands of cars proudly display U.S. flags. Many overpasses have a flag draped over the side. September 11 has unified Americans like no other event in recent history.

We are not only American citizens, but also citizens of the kingdom of God. "Our citizenship is in heaven, from which we also eagerly wait for a Savior, the Lord Jesus Christ" (Phil. 3:20, NASB). We are citizens of both America and heaven. The important questions are, "Where is our primary citizenship and loyalty? Are we first Americans and then Christians? Or are we first Christians and then Americans?"

During these tragic times, we respond and react with many emotions. We are shocked. We feel victimized. We grieve. We are appalled. We are angry that innocent lives were lost. We want justice. We want retaliation. We fear an uncertain future.

Our reaction to this crisis, however, shows how we view our loyalties and our primary citizenship. We may say we are primarily Christians, and then Americans, but do our responses and our attitudes reflect those priorities?

During a time of national crisis such as this, it is easy to put our American citizenship ahead of our heavenly citizenship. We live on American soil, and so we identify with suffering and grieving in our land. The media's spin on these events also influences our attitudes about our earthly citizenship.

I think we should read the *Heavenly Post* before we pick up the *Washington Post*. If we give first attention to the media's influence before we immerse ourselves in the Word of God, we may elevate America above Christianity.

Our primary loyalty is also revealed in the way we talk to others about this situation. Do we include ourselves when we refer to the United States' response or the government's plan of action? If so, I fear our primary loyalty is shifting toward our American citizenship. As we identify with the USA, it blurs our distinctiveness as nonresistant Christians.

In discussing these issues, we should use words that do not unreservedly identify us with our government. We can discuss what "our government" or "our country" or "the United States" is planning rather than what "we" are doing.

Let us carefully consider our relationship with our country. We contradict ourselves when we identify closely with America's military goals and yet call ourselves peacemakers. As a nonresistant Christian, my primary loyalty must be to the kingdom of God. I cannot say what the proper response of our government should be in this time of crisis. God has ordained government to keep order (Rom. 13). Thus it is responsible for the "punishment of evildoers" (1 Pet. 2:14, NASB). Though we do not always understand the ways of God, I am thankful that God's ways are superior to ours.

David E. Nisly is Vice President of Finance for Choice Books of Northern Virginia. From an article in Calvary Messenger, *November 2001.*

Which God Blesses America?

Donald B. Kraybill

In the aftermath of the terrible events of September 11, God has suddenly become popular. Across the land, bumper stickers, marquee signs, and banners proclaim, GOD BLESS AMERICA. At sporting events, political gatherings, worship services, and civic meetings, people are singing "God Bless America," our new national anthem. Does God really bless America? What do we mean by this phrase that has united so many Americans? And to which God do we sing?

Layers of meaning pack this pithy phrase. For some, it is a prayer of affirmation that welcomes God's smile upon the land of the free and the brave. For others, the blessing means that God endorses and supports our military ventures. The phrase can also be a plea for divine blessing: "Please, Lord God, give us a divine okay." From campfires to parades, the words may yearn for spiritual guidance, pleading for God to help us find our way in these dark days, or asking God to protect us from future terrorists' attacks.

And I suspect that for many of us, especially in recent days, it is a cry to aid the suffering, beseeching God to comfort those pained by injury, loss, or ethnic profiling. Regardless of its meaning, the phrase has evoked some of our deepest emotions to blend God and country together.

To receive God's blessing is the ultimate congratulation, filled with divine sanction and solidarity. We cannot find a higher blessing. Yet "God Bless America" can be an empty slogan, filled with any meaning. What do we mean by *bless?* Does *America* mean the people? The government? Are we asking for warm heavenly fuzzies, or truly seeking divine guidance?

The bland sense easily invites distortion. It can even become idolatrous if we use the slogan to justify anything our nation does. Then "God" shrinks to a socially constructed puppet that merely reflects our human fears and feelings.

A tribal god smiles on everything its nation does. When god becomes a national mascot, god cheers military action in the name of justice or anything politically expedient at the moment. While it may reassure us that we are God's pet nation, other countries have their own tribal gods cheering them on as well. Thus wars turn into "holy" conflicts, with tribal gods applauding on both sides of the trenches. Peoples and nations alike hunger for divine approval and blessing, and those inclinations easily lead to national idolatry in the name of god.

When public piety is surging, Christians must distinguish between the god of American civil religion and the God revealed in Jesus of Nazareth. The God of Jesus sends rain on the just and the unjust. This God urges us to love our enemies, bless those who curse us, render to no one evil for evil, and leave vengeance to Heaven (Matt. 5). This God tells us to forgive seventy times seven (18:22). Suffering torture at the hands of terrorists, Jesus said, "Father, forgive them; for they do not know what they are doing" (Luke 23:34).

The God of the Christian faith so loved the entire world that he sought to redeem it (John 3:16). For this God, there is no east and west, no political borders, no pet nations. The kingdom of this God is a global family that transcends national boundaries. This God blesses the poor in spirit, the outcasts, the stigmatized, the impoverished, and those who suffer. This God walks in the valley of the shadow of death with all who are traumatized with fear (Ps. 23:4). Is this the God we worship when we sing "God Bless America," or is it a tribal god, the golden calf of American nationalism?

This is not a plea for ingratitude for the many blessings of our country. I am abundantly grateful to live in a country that provides freedom of religion, freedom of the press, and respect for dissenting voices like mine. I give thanks for a stable economic and political system. I am thankful for a nation that provides economic opportunity and legal protection for all persons, regardless of race, religion, or class. These are precious blessings for which I am extremely grateful.

I'm also sure God's blessing was showered on the heroic firefighters, police officers, and others who gave their lives in rescue efforts on September 11. God surely blesses the millions of acts of charity and compassion extended to those who caught the brunt of the suffering. God surely blesses the prayer and singing that pulled many Americans together in new ways, above old divisions of politics, race, and religion.

In all of these ways, God blesses us as people. My point however, is simply this: I do not think it is appropriate to talk or sing about God blessing military action. The God revealed in Jesus of Nazareth does not bless or sanction military action. If the leaders of the nation deem that military action is necessary, I prefer that they not mislead us by sugarcoating violence with a blessing from a tribal god. To do that is to profane the name of god—to abuse the name of god—in the same way that military leaders, over the centuries, have done whenever they needed a divine blessing on campaigns of violence.

Donald B. Kraybill *is Professor of Sociology and Anabaptist Studies at Messiah College, Grantham, Pennsylvania.*

"God Bless . . ."

David E. Ortman

Ever since September 11, a chorus of "God Bless Ameica" has swept the nation. What does this say about ourselves versus the world? Just once, I'd like to hear a chorus of "God bless Australia." Or "God Bless Afghanistan."

If God is a great God, then surely God is big enough to bless all the people of the world. Or is our God too small?

Here is my effort at a new version:

> God bless the world you made,
> All people here.
> Stand beside us and guide us,
> From Afghanistan to Zaire.
> From the mountains, to the prairies,
> To the oceans, white with foam,
> God bless the world you made,
> Our home sweet home.
> God bless the world you made,
> Our home sweet home.

David E. Ortman lives in Seattle, Washington.

Reflections on "Finlandia"

Jeff Gundy

The problem with patriotism and flag-waving, it seems to me, isn't love of country, but "love" that gets coupled with hatred and mistrust of other countries and people. So I'd be happier if, after people say "God bless America," they'd also say "And God bless us all." God knows we all need it.

The song "Finlandia"—from Finland of course—shows that people everywhere both desire and deserve the right to love their countries. The second verse goes like this:

> My country's skies are bluer than the ocean,
> And sunlight shines on clover leaf and pine.
> But other lands have sunlight too and clover,
> And skies are ev'rywhere as blue as mine.
> O hear my prayer, O gods of all the nations,
> A song of peace for their lands and for mine.

Jeff Gundy teaches and writes poetry at Bluffton (Ohio) College.

My Struggle with the Flag

Paul Keim

In the wake of the September 11 events, I began to wonder about my identity as an American. How it feels. How it is expressed. As the nation reeled in shock and grief, I found it difficult to explain, even to myself, my conflicted feelings of anguish and anger on one hand, and on the other hand my desire for understanding and reconciliation.

Might it be possible, I asked myself, to join other Americans in expressing solidarity in this case—even using the flag to symbolize my sense of grief and loss, to express compassion and care? Not to do so seemed to concede the symbol of the flag to those who advocate violence and bigotry. In these circumstances, my aversion to this national symbol feels like a lost opportunity, and perhaps even a failure of responsibility.

My family has lived in this country for seven generations. I anticipate that my children and descendants will live here. I don't want them to be fully assimilated into the values of this culture. I don't want them to find their primary identity in being American. I want them to feel like citizens of the world.

But there are values here that I hope they continue to affirm: freedom of conscience, separation of church and state, the rule of law, and representational government.

These are not exclusively American values, nor are they particularly biblical. But they have been realized in this country, I think, in a unique way: A way to be affirmed. A way benefiting me and generations of my family. A way envied by millions of people around the world. A way that could and should be guaranteed for all people.

Thus, I put a small picture of an American flag on my office door here at Goshen College. I realize there's a risk in using this symbol. Perhaps it is beyond redemption for Anabaptist-Mennonite Christians. But before I am willing to concede that, I feel a duty to try to use it in a different way.

After the bombing of Afghanistan started, I took the flag off my door. I did not want to be identified in any way with this violent retaliation. The incessant invoking of God's blessing on the nation by political and religious leaders now seemed blasphemous. I was sure that the bombing would only perpetuate the cycle of violence in our world. No matter what its outcome in the short term, it will not restore our lost sense of security. It will not bring about peace based on justice. I hoped to wash my hands of the guilt of shed blood.

But recently I put the flag up again, reluctantly, along with a written explanation. I know that now more than ever the American flag symbolizes repression and military muscle to many people around the world. My display of the flag is intended partly as an admission that I share responsibility for that. I cannot hide my complicity behind an attitude of political detachment and moral superiority. My taxes help pay for militarism (even when I practice war-tax resistance, and the money is taken involuntarily).

I will display the flag, for now, and try to exhibit an alternative patriotism: One that combines love of country with love for all God's children. One that admits and even celebrates the greatness of this land with a conscience pricked by the evils it does in my name. One informed by Hebrew prophets who witnessed to their nation and its leaders, while expressing loving care and concern for the well-being of its people.

Paul Keim *is Professor of Biblical Studies at Goshen (Ind.) College.*

Why I Don't Fly Old Glory

Valerie Weaver-Zercher

Never has the American flag been as chic as in the months following September 11. Like acorns that pile up in the fall, flags seem to be dropping from the sky and landing everywhere: from flower boxes and sofa covers to roadwork signs and my neighbor's pants. "These colors don't run," proclaim T-shirts, with flags rippling across their fronts.

Christian people across the nation are often among the proudest flag-flyers. Old Glory hangs in many churches, suggesting that Christians must unite behind their government and support their leaders with prayer and military service, if need be. Christians are also among those who refuse to display the flag. At a public prayer service for peace at the Pennsylvania State Capitol, on the day the United States started bombing Afghanistan, the only flag was one held by a counter-protester. He jeered at those gathered, "Not a flag among you! You must be Osama bin Laden's fan club!"

Funny how a piece of fabric can arouse such strong feelings. Indeed, that the flag is a *symbol* is what makes the discussion so tricky. Symbols, by definition, represent something else; they stand in place of an idea, a feeling, a story. So while the symbol itself remains static—a flag is a flag is a flag—the thoughts and emotions that it evokes are multiple and shifting.

In a discussion with a friend, I realized the power of symbols. To her, flying a flag during a national crisis is a sign of mourning, of solidarity with the people who lost loved ones in the terrorist attacks, of identity with a homeland, of rootedness in her neighborhood, town, and country. Even though she disagrees with her government at times, the flag symbolizes her solidarity with neighbors and connections with a place.

For me, it's a different story. I cannot fly the American flag because to me, it is first a symbol of militarism. It is a sign of the wars that our government has waged to protect our economic and political interests at the expense of other peoples of the world. The wars have always resulted in the loss of life that military strategists call "collateral damage."

The flag reminds me of more than 100,000 people killed when my country dropped atomic bombs on Hiroshima and Nagasaki. It reminds me that military spending will devour 47 percent of the federal budget in 2002. It makes me think of husbands, sisters, fathers, and aunts being killed and killing others under orders from their government.

To me, the flag also symbolizes my country's overuse of global resources. We of the USA use more than our fair share of global resources. We consume twice as much energy per person as citizens of other industrialized nations, and 351 times as much as the average Ethiopian. The government of our rich nation allocates a lower percentage of our gross national product to foreign aid than any other Western nation.

To me, the flag profoundly symbolizes nationalism, that commitment to nation that eclipses one's commitment to anything or anyone else—such as God, family, the world. The flag asks for a complete allegiance I cannot give, because I am first of all a citizen under the reign of God. So even while I live in this nation, I am a stranger within it.

Many of my actions answer the calls of both my country and Christ, such as taking food to a sick neighbor, giving money to my local fire department, or tutoring neighborhood kids. But what do I do when my country declares war? What can I do when my country's sanctions lead to the deaths of 500,000 Iraqi infants? At these moments my citizenship under God's reign must trump that of my nation. I must find ways to walk in Christ's way of peace rather than my nation's way of war.

Don't misunderstand: I am grateful for many values of this country, especially freedom of speech and freedom to worship. Following September 11, I found a new, deep sense of solidarity with my fellow citizens. As a friend said to me, "I think this week we learned that we're Americans."

But many questions remain for me: How can I express my solidarity with both my fellow citizens and the people suffering in Afghanistan, Iraq, and other countries? How can I symbolize my commitment to peace in a nation hell-bent on warmaking? How can I live as a faithful servant of Christ, who calls me to love and action, regardless of national boundaries?

I don't know how to answer all these questions, but I do know that they make it difficult for me to fly a flag. As North American Christians, we must disentangle ourselves from civil religion, the fusion of Christianity and patriotism, invoking God's name to bless our nation and all its actions. Civil religion helps politicians because it turns critique of governmental actions into sin, or a sign of disrespect for God.

We must always be cautious when Caesar quotes Scripture.

If God is on our side, we can justify killing Afghans, starving Iraqi babies, and consuming more than our fair share of global resources. If God is on our side, we can justify just about anything. Patriotic religion nurtures an unquestioning narcissism of nation-love, not the costly discipleship of Christ.

Churches, then, should be a haven from the kind of nationalism that flares up during times of war. We declare allegiance, not to a god of tribal loyalty, who fights on the side of "us" against "them," but to a God who embraces all people. So although the flag represents different things to different people, an America flag in a church sanctuary signals a dangerous brew of nation and faith. The visible symbols in church should remind us of Christ's way of suffering and love, not Caesar's way of revenge. A cross, a dove, a globe, or a basin and towel point more appropriately to Christ's compassionate, peaceful lifestyle.

We need a new body of symbols for Christians who want to show their solidarity with fellow citizens and their allegiance to Christ's way of peace. In this spirit, in this search for new symbols of Christian citizenship, I offer some ideas for congregations and individuals who struggle with the flag.

Discuss your feelings about the flag. Ask people in your congregation and community to describe emotions they feel when they look at an American flag. Listen to what they say, and speak honestly about your own responses. Open up a dialogue in your church about the flag. How has your denomination or congregation related to the flag? Discuss the topic with individuals and in small group settings.

Use alternative symbols of mourning and solidarity with those who are suffering. Design a flag with a picture of the globe or a dove, for example. Display a rainbow-colored ribbon to show your solidarity with people across the world, or a black ribbon to show your grief during a tragedy. Make a banner with phrases like "United in Grief, Not in War." Erect a "Peace Pole" on your church grounds, with the word "peace" carved in various languages.

Display flags from various countries. This will symbolize your citizenship in the United States *and* the world. A church could display flags of its congregants' countries, or of nations where the church has mission and service workers. (Small flags from UN-member countries are available from the UN Gift Centre; telephone 800-860-7752.)

Speak to your elected representatives if they seek to legislate allegiance to the flag. During wartime, politicians are tempted to mandate loyalty to country, including pledging allegiance to the flag. A bill before the Pennsylvania legislature in October 2001 called for every school classroom to display a flag, and every teacher to lead students in the Pledge of Allegiance or the national anthem. Christians who believe in Christ's way of peace must inform their elected representatives about why such a rule might force them to choose between violating the law or their conscience.

Such ideas, including the choice not to display a flag, will be unpopular in the aftermath of national tragedies and during wartime. Some may view a refusal to show allegiance to the flag as silly or even as treasonous. Yet by using symbols other than the flag to express solidarity with those who suffer, at home and abroad, Christians can witness to the boundless love of a God who dwells both within and beyond our nation.

Valerie Weaver-Zercher is a freelance writer of Harrisburg, Pennsylvania. She has served as an editor of Gospel Herald.

A Flag in Worship?

Ralph Detrick

I believe it is never appropriate to have a U.S. flag at a worship service. The church is the body of Christ. The "God-with-us" whom we know in Jesus Christ is a universal God.

When we gather for worship, we are a segment of the body of Christ that stretches around the globe. The body of Christ is never aligned with partiality to any human-made geographic location. God does not "bless America" above any other of God's children.

The citizenship of a Christian is always to the universal body of Christ and only secondarily to the country in which one resides. My love of country is always subordinate to allegiance to Christ.

Ralph Detrick co-pastors the Elizabethtown (Pa.) Church of the Brethren. Adapted from a letter to the Messenger.

Faith and the Flag at Work

Titus Peachey

On September 18, a week after the attacks in New York, Washington (D.C.), and western Pennsylvania, Jim and John Smucker made a difficult decision. These owners of a group of food and lodging businesses in Lancaster County, Pennsylvania, decided not to display the U.S. flag at their businesses.

Flags had suddenly appeared both outside and inside their establishments. They asked their managers to remove the flags and explained why in a memo to employees.

The Smucker brothers respect the flag as a symbol of democracy, freedom, common identity, unity, and a constitution and government under the rule of law. But they recognized that after September 11, the flag also symbolized preparation for military action. Flying the flag could be construed to mean that they would be in support of, and stand behind, any action our government would take.

Deeply committed to Jesus' way of peace and reconciliation, they wanted to support acts of healing and restoration, not acts of war where more innocent lives would be lost. Their decision not to fly the flag reflected their personal faith and the long-standing tradition of the Mennonite congregations where they worshiped.

Within hours, they had a crisis on their hands. Phone calls and e-mails from employees expressed outrage, disbelief, and embarrassment. Even long-term employees were angry and ready to abandon the company. Managers from various sites reported intense reactions to the decision.

Valuing their relationships with their employees, the Smucker brothers decided to listen. All day Friday, September 21, from 9:00 a.m. until 9:30 p.m., Jim and John met with employees. Emotions were raw. It was a tough day.

"To many employees, our decision not to fly the flag was an insult," noted Jim. "They saw the flag as a sign of respect for those who died, especially the firefighters and policemen involved in the rescue efforts. The flag was a symbol of sympathy for families who lost loved ones. It was a sign of unity when the country was threatened. It symbolized all the freedoms we enjoy and want to keep. Our decision about the flag was misunderstood. It communicated that we don't care about these things. But these are things that we also value."

Other employees saw the flag as a symbol of U.S. military power and resolve to fight, confirming the Smuckers' own concerns. At the end of the day, the dilemma remained. Few opinions had changed, but many relationships were on a path toward healing. Mutual respect and understanding, at least, had been restored.

For Jim and John, the flag still conflicts with their ultimate allegiance to God and commitment to Christ's way of peace. But in the end, the Smuckers granted the managers at each site the freedom to make their own decisions, and flags are now on display at most of their business locations.

"We have invested many years in developing a culture where our employees are involved in decision-making processes," said John. "An atmosphere of openness and mutual respect guides our daily work. We want our employees to feel ownership of the workplace community we are all helping to create. When we took the flag away, we removed a symbol important to them without involving them in the decision. We decided that our personal convictions on this issue could be subservient to the intense desires of 400 other people with whom we share our daily workplace."

During national and international crisis, when the stakes are high and emotions are raw, battle lines form quickly around the symbols and words we care deeply about. The clash is genuine. Different paths lead to different outcomes. The Smucker brothers' experience highlights two values desperately needed in these times: the courage to act on our convictions, and the courage to listen to those who disagree.

Titus Peachey is director of Peace Education for the Mennonite Central Committee U.S.

Why I Want to Wear Black

Carl F. Bowman

The headlines on Monday troubled me: "Bush Vows Crusade." "U.S. Will Rid the World of Evildoers." "Bush Warns of a Wrathful, Shadowy, and Inventive War."

The font was large and black, very black. On my way to work at Bridgewater College, National Public Radio reported America's eagerness for military action. Flags waved on Dinkel Avenue as I entered the small but growing town.

The words, "God," "American," and "War" filled public discourse, wrapping themselves around one another, multiplying, and drowning out other words that might brave the cacophony. Amid the chatter, the flexing of muscles, and the reports of college males wanting to sign up to "get some towel-heads," I experienced once again how my Brethren pacifist upbringing sets me apart.

One thing I know is that when others are wearing red, white, and blue, I want to wear black.

Black to mourn an Islamic extremism so sure of its own truth and the evil it confronts that it can rip apart bodies and relationships in the name of God. Black to mourn expressions and distortions of American patriotism that might do the same, in the name of ridding the world of evildoers. Black to mourn with the wives and children and parents of those who died in the Twin Towers, in the Pentagon, and in Pennsylvania. Black to mourn for American Muslims who will endure increased violence and fears of violence at the hands of well-meaning but misguided superpatriots. And black to mourn for those whose skin color will easily be mistaken as Middle Eastern, making them targets of hatred.

Carl F. Bowman is Professor of Sociology at Bridgewater (Va.) College. Adapted from an essay in the Daily News-Record, *Harrisonburg, Virginia.*

Is Peace Patriotic?

Paul Schrag

As a national rallying cry in these difficult days, "United we stand" is almost as popular as "God bless America."

United in sorrow? In anger? For justice? For war? In solidarity with fellow citizens? All of the above? "United we stand" calls for a conformity that pervades American patriotism in a time of crisis. To disagree with any part of the slogan's assumed message would be, well, un-American.

What about those not united behind military action? We do stand united behind some of the slogan's meanings. We share the nation's sorrow and a desire that the murderers be brought to justice. Yet we can't help but think that the most common meaning, the one by which true patriotism is judged, is support for military action. We wish this were not so, because dissent can be patriotic.

If patriotism means wanting what is best for one's country, and if one firmly believes that waging war will not make

Americans safer or create a more just world, then advocating for peace is actually an act of patriotism.

Tolerance of dissent and respect for a diversity of beliefs are among America's most cherished ideals. The United States has not always lived up to these principles. But in many ways throughout its history, our country has moved closer to them. One example is the treatment of conscientious objectors. They were persecuted during World War I but gained recognition of their rights before World War II.

Religious minorities, including members of the historic peace churches, are grateful for these American ideals. Such principles require even greater diligence in a time of war, when the pressures to conform are high.

Responsible patriotism is not blind. Loyal citizens should ask tough questions and sometimes may raise troubling issues, recognizing that the country faces difficult choices.

Many Americans acknowledge that the country has not always made good decisions about war and peace—think of Vietnam. If citizens who call for a quick use of force are considered patriotic, should not other citizens, who believe restraint is in the national interest, also be heard?

For many pacifist Christians, love of our country is part of the reason why we want our nation to seek justice nonviolently in response to the evil showered on us on September 11. There is much to love about America and much to criticize. Everyone knows that a good citizen does both of these things. The nation can show the strength of its democratic principles by respecting diverse beliefs, including opposition to war.

Just as Christians can exemplify a patriotism without militarism, we also should avoid linking religious faith and nationalism. The body of Christ, says 1 Peter 2:9, is "a holy nation." Our citizenship in this spiritual nation—our membership in the universal church—is far more important than our citizenship in any earthly nation.

A Christian's allegiance belongs to the kingdom of God. Some, therefore, choose not to say a pledge of loyalty to any nation of this world. Such a pledge might compromise their allegiance to God, whose love knows no political borders.

Certainly it is possible to say a pledge of loyalty or to sing "God Bless America" without turning the nation into an idol and without endorsing war. After all, symbolic acts mean different things to different people. But when the nation is at war, flags are waved more often, and God-and-country songs flourish. We can sing "God Bless America" and mean it as a prayer that God will lead our nation in the ways of peace and bless other nations as well. But our neighbors will not know that is what we mean unless our words and actions clarify our symbols.

In these days, Christians need to model an inclusive patriotism, demonstrating that love of country and love of enemies are not contradictory. We can also model a humble patriotism, one that does not exaggerate our goodness and does not assume that God blesses our battles.

This kind of patriotism recognizes that, though it is natural and good for people to love their homeland, God loves the people of all nations equally. This patriotism refuses to hold the flag in religious reverence. It prays that God will bless Afghanistan as much as America.

While many Americans' religious faith intertwines with patriotism and militarism, another voice, another prayer, must also be spoken. It is the voice of those whose love for their country, and for the people of all countries, leads them to pray that the cycle of bloodshed will stop. It is a prayer that their country, though justified to wage war according to conventional ways of thinking, will see that violence itself is the enemy. This is our faint hope, but still our prayer.

Jesus summed up the wisdom and righteousness of not taking vengeance: "All who take the sword will perish by the sword" (Matt. 26:52). Violence begets more violence and intensifies hate. It cannot end until someone has the courage to stop taking an eye for an eye (5:38-48). Terrorism thrives on hate—exactly what a military response will feed.

We do not expect the government to adopt the peaceful ways of Jesus. But we can expect the government to do what serves its people best. The weapons of war that we trust for our defense were useless against the hijackers. An investment in better airport security could have saved many lives—something no bomb or missile can ever do.

America proclaims its trust in God, a God who says, "Vengeance is mine" (Deut. 32:35), who "makes wars cease to the ends of the earth," and "breaks the bow and shatters the spear" (Ps. 46:9). Now we have the opportunity to rise above the evil done to us and prove where our real trust lies.

Paul Schrag is editor of Mennonite Weekly Review. *Adapted from editorials, September 20, October 11 and 18, 2001.*

The Highest Form of Patriotism

Dale W. Brown

I question the repetitious presence of "God Bless America" in our national speech. It sounds as if we are giving God orders instead of seeking God's will for our responses.

Limiting God's blessing to America seems to be nationalistic and overpatriotic.

The purpose of *Yahweh's* blessing in Genesis 12:1-3 was a promise that through Abram's descendants all peoples of the earth would be blessed. The "God bless America" slogan shapes our prayers in ways that lack any humility. Jesus praised the tax collector who beat his breast, saying, "God, be merciful to me, a sinner!" (Luke 18:13).

In his diary, nineteenth-century Brethren martyr John Kline wrote,

> My highest conception of patriotism is found in those who love God with all heart, mind, and strength, and neighbors as themselves. Out of these affections spring the subordinate love for one's country; love truly virtuous for one's companion and children, relatives and friends, and in its most comprehensive sense taking in the whole human family.

Dale W. Brown *is a longtime peace advocate in the Church of the Brethren.*

Chapter 7

Another Way of Responding

If not war, then what?

Few of us are content to sit on the sidelines during a time of national crisis and bury our heads in the sands of despair. But it is one thing to decry the use of violence from the sidelines, and another matter altogether to generate creative alternatives that will balance the needs for both justice and security.

The writers in chapter 7 offer a variety of ways to respond to the events of September 11. These range from specific proposals for national policy to small informal steps at the local level. Virtually all the essays point to the fact that we are citizens of a larger global family. As we seek nonviolent alternatives to war, we must respect the dignity of the traditions and cultures of the larger global family. The chapter concludes with some stories of faith and hope and "A Prayer to End the Terror."

The Challenge of Terror

John Paul Lederach

Stranded for eight days while returning from Colombia to my Virginia home, I penned these observations. They are drawn from twenty years of mediating in violent situations around the globe, where cycles of revenge seem bent on perpetuating themselves and where movements find ways to justify their part in that cycle.

Consider these four ways to understand the events of September 11:

1. Understand the root of the anger. How do people reach this level of anger, hatred, and frustration? Anger of this sort—generational, identity-based anger—builds over time through a combination of events, a threat to identity, and experiences of sustained exclusion. Our response to the attacks will affect whether we reinforce and provide the soil, seeds, and nutrients for future cycles of revenge and violence, or whether the cycle changes.

We should avoid doing what such terrorists expect—the giant lashing out against the weak, the many against the few. This will only reinforce their ability to perpetrate the myth that they are under threat, fighting an irrational and mad system that has never taken them seriously and wishes to destroy them and their people. We need to destroy their myth, not their people.

2. Understand the organization. Over the years of working to promote durable peace in situations of deep, sustained vio-

lence, I have discovered one consistent purpose about the nature of movements that use violence: *Sustain yourself*. This is done through a number of approaches, but generally it is through decentralization of power and structure, secrecy, small cells, and refusal to pursue the conflict on the terms of the enemy.

Such is the genius of people like Osama bin Laden. He understands the power of a free and open system and has used it to his benefit. The enemy is not located in a territory but has entered our system. One does not conquer such an enemy by shooting at it. One responds by strengthening the system for immunity and preventing the virus.

Our greatest threat is not in Afghanistan but in our own backyard. We are not going to bomb Travelocity, Hertz Rent a Car, or an airline training school in Florida. We must move beyond the reaction to duke it out with the bad guy, or we risk creating the environment that sustains and reproduces the very virus we wish to prevent.

3. Remember that realities are constructed. Conflict happens when people construct different perceptions of reality. We see the other side as fanatics, madmen, irrational. But from their point of view, they are not mad or irrational. Their views are reinforced by years of superpower struggle that used or excluded them, encroaching Western values their religion considers immoral, or an enemy image overwhelmingly powerful, bombing others, and always seeming to win. So they construct a rational worldview of a heroic struggle against evil. We do it, and so do they.

The way to break such a cycle of justified violence is to step outside of it. This starts with understanding that TV sound bites about madmen and evil are not good bases for policy. The most significant impact we can make on terrorists' ability for sustaining their view of us as evil is to change their perception of who we are by responding in unexpected ways. This will take courage and leadership capable of envisioning a horizon of change.

4. Understand recruitment. The greatest power of terror is the ability to regenerate itself. Yet political leaders wishing to end the violence believe they can do it by getting rid of the perpetrator of the violence. That may have been the lesson of multiple centuries, but it is not the lesson from the past thirty years. When people feel threat, exclusion, and direct violence, their greatest effort is placed on survival.

These movements show an extraordinary capacity for regenerating chosen myths and renewed struggle. We should try to remove the channels, justifications, and sources that attract and sustain recruitment into violent activities. None of the perpetrators in the recent attacks were much older than forty, and many were half that age. This is the reality we face: Recruitment happens on a sustained basis. Military force will not stop it.

Open warfare will create the soils in which terrorism grows. Military action to destroy terror, particularly as it affects already-vulnerable civilian populations, will be like clubbing a gone-to-seed dandelion head. We will only sustain the myth of why we are evil and will assure yet another generation of recruits.

Now consider three things that could have a much greater impact than seeking accountability through revenge:

1. Energetically pursue a sustainable peace in the Israeli-Palestinian conflict. The United States has much it can do to support and make this process work. We should bring the same energy to building an international coalition for peace in this conflict that we have pursued in building international coalitions for war, particularly in the Middle East.

Create a whole new view of what we stand for as a

nation. Rather than fighting terror with force, we could remove one of their most coveted elements: the soils of generational conflict, perceived as unjust that are used to perpetrate hatred and recruitment.

The biggest blow we can serve terror is to make it irrelevant. The worst thing we can do is to feed it by making it and its leaders the center stage of what we do.

2. *Invest financially in development, education, and a broad social agenda in countries surrounding Afghanistan, rather than destroying the Taliban in a search for bin Laden.* The greatest pressure we could put on bin Laden would be to remove the source of his justifications and alliances. We should ask countries like Pakistan, Tajikistan, and even Iran and Syria, a strategic question: How can we help you meet the fundamental needs of your people?

To prevent terrorism from reproducing itself, we must develop quality relationships with whole regions, peoples, and worldviews. If we strengthen those relationships, we weaken and eventually eliminate the soil where terror germinates. Let's do the unexpected. Let's create new strategic alliances never before thought possible.

3. *Pursue a diplomatic but dynamic support of the Arab League (a voluntary association of Arabic-speaking countries) to address the root causes of discontent.* We should seek to create a web of ethics, built from the heart and soul of all traditions, to uproot violence in their own traditions.

Rather than convincing others that our way of life, religion, or structure of governance is better, we should be honest about the sources of violence in our own house and invite others to do the same. Through genuine dialogue, we can show that life-giving ethics are rooted in the core of all peoples. This will have a far greater impact in reducing terror for our children's children than any amount of military action can possibly muster.

In summary, change the game again. We need to think differently about the challenges of terror. We must not give the movements we deplore gratuitous fuel for self-regeneration, fulfilling their prophecies by providing them with martyrs and justifications.

They changed the game, entered our lives, our homes, and our workplaces, and turned our own tools to our demise. We will not win this struggle for justice, peace, and human dignity with the traditional weapons of war. We need to change the game again. Let us give birth to the unexpected.

John Paul Lederach is Professor of International Peacebuilding at the Joan B. Kroc Institute for International Peace, University of Notre Dame, and Distinguished Scholar, Eastern Mennonite University. Adapted from an essay in The Mennonite, *October 2, 2001, that was taken from a longer version available on the Kroc Institute's website: www.nd.edu, select Offices, then Kroc Institute.*

If Not Military Force and War, Then What?

The Friends Committee on National Legislation

If not military force and war, then what *should* the United States do to respond to these horrific attacks against innocent

civilians? The United States must not sacrifice its core values while defending them from acts of terror. Rather, the USA should prove its enduring commitment to freedom, democracy, human rights, and the rule of law in the ways it responds to these acts of terror and pursues justice.

For example, we recommend that the U.S. government:

1. Mobilize and lead law enforcement agencies around the world to investigate, apprehend, and bring to justice those responsible, to the full extent of U.S. and international law. To advance international cooperation, the U.S. Senate should immediately ratify and implement the International Convention for the Suppression of Terrorist Bombing.

2. Preserve civil liberties, maintain full public accountability of U.S. governing institutions, and protect vulnerable U.S. minorities from hate crimes and harassment, against Arab-Americans, Muslims, and others.

3. Lead the UN in cooperative action to interrupt and seize the financial resources that support these criminal terror networks. To support this effort, the U.S. Senate should promptly ratify and implement the International Convention on the Suppression of the Financing of Terrorism.

4. Lead the UN in bringing diplomatic, political, and economic pressure to bear against the governing regimes of nations that give support or shelter to terror networks. If international sanctions are applied, they should be focused narrowly on those in political power.

5. Respond with compassion and generous aid to the suffering of innocent peoples in Iraq, the Sudan, Afghanistan, Pakistan, and other countries, even if their governments are found to support terror networks. For example, shower Afghanistan with humanitarian aid, not bombs.

6. Resume and intensify U.S. efforts to secure a just and

lasting peace in the Israeli-Palestinian conflict, a major source of deep anti-U.S. sentiment throughout the Arab world.

7. Lead the international community in cooperative efforts to reduce stockpiles of chemical, biological, and nuclear weapons/materials in the USA, Russia, and elsewhere, and guard against unauthorized use. Support increased funding for the "Nunn-Lugar" threat-reduction initiative.

8. Support an international ban on the sale and transfer of weapons to zones of conflict. Weapons sales and transfers increase acts of violence, suffering, and the collapse of civil social institutions. The USA is the world's largest exporter of weapons. It should not export weapons to regimes that are undemocratic and violate human rights.

9. Dramatically increase U.S. humanitarian aid to refugees in zones of conflict, now numbering in the millions. War orphans, refugee children, and youth are especially vulnerable to recruitment by terrorist organizations. This is of special concern today in Afghanistan and Central Asia.

10. Assist individuals and families in the United States who have lost wage earners or jobs as a result of the attack and its economic aftermath.

War is not the answer.

The Friends Committee on National Legislation. *Adapted from "Talking Points," September 26, 2001.*

God's People and a Different Way

Gerald Biesecker-Mast

In the wake of September 11, the Christian church should seek to present the world and its powers with persuasive alternatives to the violent course of action pursued by the U.S. government and its allies in Afghanistan.

We can note the long-term danger of giving money and weapons to unscrupulous political movements who happen for the moment to have the same enemy as the United States. We can also protest the killing of innocent civilians or even of members of the Taliban who are not directly responsible for the September 11 attacks. We can urge the USA to view the struggle against terrorism less as a military campaign and more as a judicial proceeding. We can note that by engaging in military action, the USA perpetuates the cycle of violence and reprisals. We can urge the USA to seek for a just settlement of the Israeli occupation of Palestine.

All of these practical policy suggestions and more should lead to public witness from Christian pacifists. We may believe that reducing violence is an effective public policy in most instances. Nevertheless, we must remember what is most basic: our commitment to peace rests in Jesus Christ and is dependent on the Holy Spirit's power, not the pragmatics of diplomacy and foreign policy.

We also should note that most of the plausible alternatives

to military violence (such as an international tribunal or diplomatic initiatives) involve at least the threat of violence and coercion and thus fall outside the bounds of biblical pacifism. Yet we can acknowledge that such judicial and diplomatic alternatives are nonetheless better than military violence. In a world that does not assume or accept the grace and power of Jesus Christ, we believe that God's providence (if not God's will) extends to practices and policies that do not recognize and follow Christ's perfection.

Yet we should not allow the recognition of God's providence amid war and violence to tempt us ever to argue for more violence rather than less. For example, those who are committed to biblical nonviolence should never find themselves arguing for more use of military power as an effective strategy in a fallen world. Our public arguments should always seek to reduce the use of violence, even when we are not making an explicit argument for complete pacifism for everyone at every public occasion.

If we believe that the rule of God in Christ is comprehensive and that the witness of the church is for the whole world, then we should always call the state to hear Christ's invitation to defenseless discipleship. The call of Christ to enemy love comes not only to members of the peace churches but also to George W. Bush and to Colin Powell and to Donald Rumsfeld. We must never contradict that call in our public witness.

In democratic societies, Christians who oppose war often still identify with public policies they oppose. Discussions may focus on "what we are doing" in Afghanistan, or military actions "we are taking" there. We do need to acknowledge our complicity in U.S. foreign policy. But it may also be time to quit using "we/our/us" collective pronouns when talking about the actions of the U.S. government, thus renouncing our identification with such policies.

When I discuss these matters, I try to talk about what "the White House" is doing, "the Pentagon," or "the Congress," rather than in terms of what "we" are doing, to distance myself from actions of violence I cannot approve.

Though I am an American citizen, it is nevertheless policymakers in Washington, D.C., who are undertaking this war, quite apart from whether I approve of it or not. In this small way, we can signal our ultimate allegiance to Jesus Christ at a time when the state and public opinion rewards public displays of patriotic loyalty. In Ohio, where I live, the state assembly is considering a law that would require the pledge of allegiance in every public school assembly.

These are times when we need to talk with our children about our conviction that the American nation is not synonymous with the reign of God, and that our loyalties are first of all with God. In times like these, the stories of our faith ancestors, who made the difficult choice to choose Christ over Caesar, become near and dear to all. May they help us remember our desire and hope for "a better country," whose "builder and maker is God" (Heb. 11:10, 16, KJV).

Gerald Biesecker-Mast is Professor of Communication at Bluffton (Ohio) College.

A Call to Faith and Action

The Mennonite Central Committee

As an agency of historic peace churches, Mennonite Central Committee (MCC) upholds the call of Jesus to love enemies and live as peacemakers. Jesus calls those who follow him to live as citizens in a new kingdom, to "seek the welfare of the city" (Jer. 29:7) where we live, and to be advocates and builders of peaceful systems and institutions. This way of living includes finding ways to love those we see as enemies and refusing to participate in war or killing.

Throughout its history, MCC has stood against a culture of violence by witnessing against war preparation, enemy demonization, and the use of military force to solve difficult international problems. At the same time, MCC has worked to build a culture of life through ministries of education, development, exchange, peacemaking, and helping people in need.

Our theological convictions and our experience around the world convince us that a campaign of military retaliation will harm many more people and perpetuate the cycle of violence. Therefore, we call all people of faith to speak out against calls for revenge and retaliation.

As people striving to follow Christ's way of peace, we will seek to build a culture of peace rather than resort to messages of retaliation and weapons of destruction.

Executive Committee, Mennonite Central Committee. From "A Call to Faith and Action: The Crisis of September 11, 2001," September 22, 2001.

Think Globally, Love Globally

Miriam Adeney

How do we respond to the devastation of September 11, the deadly attacks on the World Trade Center and the Pentagon? Many responses come to mind. Prayer. Care for the injured and bereft. Increased security, increased vigilance. Just punishment for the masterminds behind the carnage. Sharper on-the-ground intelligence gathering. Stronger international cooperation against terrorism. Congregational immersion in Scripture stories of God's people who lived through radical loss and destabilization, from Joseph to Daniel to John, Peter, and Paul. There is one more response: Christians will want to become better global citizens.

Hit in the solar plexus. Since the so-called end of the Cold War, many of us have not given much thought to the rest of the world except through occasional business, tourist, or short-term mission connections. Those days are over. We've been hit in the solar plexus with the truth that we are globally connected and cannot cut loose.

In Thomas Friedman's bestseller on globalization, *The Lexus and the Olive Tree*, he describes a label on a computer part that reads, "This part was made in Malaysia, Singapore, the Philippines, China, Mexico, Germany, the U.S., Thailand, Canada, and Japan. It was made in so many different places that we cannot specify a country of origin." We are globally integrated as never before.

Yet many of us continue to live cocooned in our own little circle of friends, walled off from people who are different. To think about the rest of the world overwhelms us. Masses of data pour out of the media, jumbled in sound bites that juxtapose great human tragedies with beer ads. We know Americans overseas have made mistakes. How can ordinary citizens like you and me know enough to make intelligent comments on global issues?

Pray through the newspaper. Christians should be different. Of all people, Christians are to love our neighbors. When our neighborhood expands to include the globe, then we're called to love globally. How? Some of the most important steps may be some of the simplest:

• Pray through the newspaper, especially the world news section.

• Befriend foreigners who live in your city.

• Develop strong relationships with your church or denominational missionaries.

• Ask members who are businesspeople to talk about their global involvements.

• Go to the local college and find out whether there's a group of local "friends of international students."

• Ask your high school and college youth what they're studying about global issues.

• Teach a church class on the biblical basis of mission, tracing global issues from Genesis to Revelation.

We should strive to do this without a patronizing smile, keeping others at arm's length. Loving our neighbors means something more. It means being vulnerable. It means entering into their pain. When God in Jesus came to live among us, he shared our troubles and felt our hurts. Do we empathize with those in other countries?

Globalization has hurt many. Though transnational business has brought much wealth to other countries, people there suspect that transnational corporations—most based in the USA—are reaping the lion's share of benefits. This breeds a love-hate feeling toward America.

Yong-Hun Jo of Korea, in "Globalization as a Challenge to the Churches in Asia Today" (*Asian Journal of Theology*, Oct. 2000), says poverty levels in Asian countries have worsened as globalization has bloomed. The article's tone is moderate, recognizing the benefits of a vigorous economy. Yet it also speaks of bankruptcies, destruction of jobs, massive unemployment, a sharp rise in prices, decline in wages, capital flight into tax-free zones, reduction of public services, environmental degradation, and a growing distance between the rich and the poor. At present, 34 percent of the children under age five in Southeast Asia are underweight, as are 50 percent of the children in South Asia. Half the people in the world live on $2 a day or less.

When labor must follow jobs in a borderless world, many leave behind spouses, children, and parents with whom they would have traditionally spent much time. Globalization obliterates family closeness.

Do we feel that pain? The prophet Amos blasted God's people because they did not grieve for hurting people:

Woe to you who are complacent in Zion,
    and to you who feel secure on Mount Samaria,
you notable men of the foremost nation. . . .
You lie on beds inlaid with ivory

> and lounge on your couches.
> You dine on choice lambs. . . .
> You . . . improvise on musical instruments. . . .
>> But you do not grieve over the ruin of Joseph.
>> (Amos 6:1-6, NIV)

The writer of James has similar concerns:

> Suppose a brother or sister is without clothes and daily food. If one of you says to him, "Go, I wish you well; keep warm and well fed," but does nothing about his physical needs, what good is it? In the same way, faith by itself, if it is not accompanied by action, is dead.
>> (James 2:13-17, NIV)

There are many macro-structural and micro-structural ways to reach out to these needs, but they are beyond the scope of this essay. Evangelism remains primary. Economic programs may teach methods, but evangelism will unleash the meaning and the motivation to use those methods conscientiously.

The healing of the nations. Our government and military is responding to the devastation of September 11 at several levels. But for cozy and complacent Christians, this tragedy has been a personal wake-up call. There's a big, real world out there. We cannot ignore the pains of other peoples without danger to ourselves—from huge hungry populations, from environmental degradation, from religious terrorism.

Becoming global Christians does not mean a paternalistic relationship with believers in other countries. It means being siblings under a heavenly Father. We have much to give in answering some needs, but our brothers and sisters have resources to share with us. We must listen to how believers in Indonesia, Sri Lanka, and Malaysia have learned to live with the constant threat of terrorism. We must learn from believers in Rwanda and Croatia about forgiving known and unknown enemies. Near Eastern believers have much to teach us about responding to extreme forms of Islam.

The earth—all of it—is the Lord's (Ps. 24:1). All of Scripture rings with this. God's concern for global issues didn't begin when Jesus said, "Go into all the world," or "You will be my witnesses" (Mark 16:15; Acts 1:8). Thousands of years earlier, Abraham heard God call his name: "I will bless you, . . . and in you all the families of the earth will be blessed" (Gen. 12:2-3).

Isaiah saw the people of God as "a light to the nations" (42:6). Habakkuk saw the earth "filled with the knowledge of the glory of the LORD, as the waters cover the sea" (2:14, NIV). Micah saw that "his greatness will reach to the ends of the earth. And he will be their peace" (5:4-5, NIV). Jonah, Daniel, Esther, Nehemiah, and even Naaman's little slave girl saw God's care for the nations.

All of Scripture resonates with God's absorbing interest in the whole earth. We cannot be healthy American Christians today and ignore the world. A global concern is not optional. It comes from God's heart.

In his brief commentary on Revelation, *For the Healing of the Nations,* Justo Gonzalez reminds us,

> We must be multicultural, not just so that those from other cultures may feel at home among us, but also so that we may feel at home in God's future, . . . because like John of Patmos, our eyes have seen the glory of the coming of the Lord; because we know and we believe that on that great waking-up morning when the stars begin to fall, when we gather at the river where angel feet have trod, we shall all, from all nations and tribes and peoples and lan-

guages, we shall all sing without ceasing: "Holy, holy, holy!"

Miriam Adeney *is editor at large for* Christianity Today *and Associate Professor of World Christian Studies at Seattle Pacific University. Adapted from an article in* Christianity Today, *October 22, 2001.*

Neighbors Around the Table

Krista Weidner

In State College, Pennsylvania, on the evening of September 26, more than 130 Christian and Muslim neighbors gathered around tables for a picnic and fellowship at a local park. In the wake of the September 11 terrorist attacks and the rhetoric of war and hate that followed, David B. Miller, pastor of University Mennonite Church (UMC), wanted to reach out in peace to Muslims in the State College and Penn State University (PSU) community.

"Too often, those of us with convictions about peacemaking tend to retreat when there's a call to arms," he said. "We believe there's nothing we can do. But I think there are nonviolent alternatives we can offer. We wanted to have this picnic as a concrete way to demonstrate the fruit of reconciliation."

David Miller sees the gathering as a small but significant act of peacemaking. "What if every Muslim in the United

States could, say, 'This is how Christians in this country have responded?' And what if each of us Christians could say, 'This has been our experience with the Muslim community?' I don't think it's overly idealistic to think we can change the world through person-to-person interactions. After all, aren't the logic and power of terrorism defeated when we refuse the world they seek to create?"

Krista Weidner lives in State College, Pennsylvania. From an article in The Mennonite, *October 23, 2001.*

Peacemakers
Need to Listen, Too

Karl S. Shelly

Voices for peace have become unwelcome in the wake of September 11. Newspaper columnists mock pacifists. Letters to the editor ridicule those who dare to speak for peace.

In the face of this rhetorical challenge, I began to feel defensive and angry. I knew who the real enemy was. It was those with whom I disagreed.

Yet in a moment of grace, I sensed the need to back away from the pitfall of self-righteousness, the trap of believing that I hold the truth and need not listen to others.

As I began to listen to the words of those calling for war, I heard three messages:

1. Don't minimize the enormity of this tragedy. Some

insist that the only remedy for the events of September 11 is to bomb the murderers and their friends "back into the Stone Age." In the face of such terrible deeds, people meet with rebuke any words from would-be peacemakers that appear to gloss over the thousands of lost lives and jump quickly to analysis. There is little patience for those who skip the stories of human suffering and the tales of heroic courage in a rush to offer solutions.

2. Don't divide us. One letter in our local newspaper said that those who won't support the war should move to Afghanistan. Underneath this intolerance of dissent, I believe, is a fervent longing for unity. We as a nation have been divided for years by political partisanship. Race and class have divided us. Now, in the wake of this tragedy, there is a strong sense that we have transcended what separates us and experienced a new connectedness as Americans.

3. Don't shortchange the call for justice. A local politician noted: "Pacifists think that what is needed is for the United States to simply make friends with the Taliban—that playing nice will dissolve anti-American terrorist cults. They (pacifists) couldn't be more misguided."

Although uninformed about nonviolent responses to violence, under this statement lies an intense desire for justice. This politician worries that those who preach love and mercy will neglect the need for justice. In essence, he is affirming the peace activists' adage: "No justice, no peace."

I need to hear these messages. And while I don't support the conclusions they draw, I can support the underlying concerns. I affirm the call to grieve deeply for the victims and salute thankfully the courage of rescue workers. I share the desire to build on our unity in our quest for peace and healing. I join the call for justice for the wrong that has happened.

I do this because these concerns are legitimate, *and* it is tactically important to do so. If we haven't acknowledged the genuine concerns of those with whom we disagree, our message doesn't have a chance. Woe to the peacemaker who does not humbly listen to the message of the opponent.

Listening does not guarantee that our concerns will be equally heard or make witnessing for peace any easier. There is even a danger that listening can become an end in itself, leaving the louder voices never challenged. A temptation to only listen can also be an excuse when those witnessing for peace are labeled unpatriotic, even evil.

But to stay silent now is to keep our light under a bushel (Matt. 5:14-15). With prayer and reflection, we must find a Spirit-led way to witness for God's peace. We must find a path that is neither self-righteous sloganeering nor immobilized listening. That path, I believe, includes speaking words of lament and comfort as the psalmist did. It includes sharing the prophetic vision that God has given us through Jesus—a vision of loving enemies, seeking justice, casting out hatred, and standing with victims wherever they are.

We are to speak this vision boldly, knowing that it holds little currency among the dominant opinion-makers in our country. We are to speak this vision sensitively, being aware of the concerns of those who disagree. We are to speak this vision confidently, assured that goodness is stronger than evil, love is stronger than hate, and life is stronger than death.

Karl S. Shelly is co-pastor of Assembly Mennonite Church, Goshen, Indiana. From an essay in Mennonite Weekly Review, *October 18, 2001.*

An Everlasting Supper

Roy Hange

In the Christian Quarter of Old Damascus, twenty yards from the street called Straight, thirteen of us gathered around the long table in the vaulted dining room of the Syrian Orthodox Seminary. Our simple evening meal began with the prayer Jesus taught in the Syriac dialect of the language Jesus spoke, Aramaic. The Lord's Prayer was lead by the spiritual director of the seminary, a gentle and wise monk named Father Issa. The English equivalent of his name is Jesus. Father Jesus sat at the head of the table, which happened to include twelve others that evening. The dining room was framed by two pictures of the Lord's Supper.

The twelve "disciples" that evening came from five nations: Iraq, Lebanon, Syria, Turkey, and the United States. There were four Christian Iraqis who had defected from the Iraqi army either during or after the Gulf War and were temporarily living at the seminary. There were several Lebanese and Syrian monks studying at the seminary along with Father Issa, who was Turkish, and myself, who was an American teaching English and studying Syriac. A visitor, also a member of the Syrian Orthodox Church, had just returned from being a soldier in one of the multinational forces stationed in Saudi Arabia during the Gulf War.

After the prayer, we shared accounts of our lives during the Gulf War. As our discussion deepened, we soon discovered we were as much a fellowship of death as we were brothers in Christ. In the midst of the visitor's stories about life with the multinational forces in Saudi Arabia, a monk observed that the visitor and the former Iraqi foot soldier sitting across the table from him could have shot each other.

I commented that my government had dropped bombs on the heads of those sitting around me—bombs that became shrapnel the doctors opposite me had pulled out of the bodies of their fellow countrymen. One of the former Iraqi ground soldiers sitting beside me had spent twenty days shaking fearfully in an underground bunker pummeled by bombs from B-52s. Once I asked him what would have happened if one of the bombs would have hit too close. He made an upward, waving motion with his hand and said, "Casper the friendly ghost." He added, "I didn't want to be a part of the war, so one day I just dropped my gun and started walking."

Two of those present were former Iraqi military doctors who had helped the victims of the war. One, stationed on the front, sent bodies back to Baghdad and the other was in a Baghdad hospital treating both military and civilian casualties. A few nights before, we had spoken about what doing triage was like for the many wounded bodies that were trucked back to Baghdad from the front.

The main air base used by allied planes in eastern Turkey was near the hometown of one of the monks. A smart bomb from a plane hit a large warehouse-like building in the northern city of Mosul. The structure was a Syrian Orthodox Church and parsonage where the wife and three children of a priest were killed. The conversation raged on—like a battle of our consciences against the sad reality we all had participated in, until an uneasy silence settled around our table.

Someone broke the silence, asking Father Issa, "Will I go

to hell?" Questions and excuses flew out of the reflective silence. "Will we be judged for this?" An Iraqi doctor said, "I never carried a gun in all my years in the military. I had no choice but to be there." Other Iraqis said they had no choice: "Either I fought, or I was shot on the spot."

One of the doctors had been assigned to witness the execution of deserters in front of their families during the Iraq-Iran war. Someone said, "I would never have shot a Christian," but the responses came back, "How would you have known whether they were Christian or not? You can't see a cross around their neck from 200 meters?"

We had gathered that evening to break bread together, even as we, through our national loyalties, had been prepared to break each other's bones a few months before. We were mortal enemies in the terms of the powers of this age, and yet brothers in the kingdom of Christ. The loyalties to the demands of those kingdoms clashed in our conversation that evening as they had in our lives a few months before.

The pictures of the Lord's Supper still framed our gathering as a silent reminder of the meaning of our supper. Near the end of our meal, I remembered Jesus' disciples during that Last Supper. They included a former tax collector and Zealots, who were enemies, sitting by one who would betray Jesus, another who would deny Jesus, and others who would flee in silence.

As I looked at the pictures once again, I imagined Jesus in their midst 1,970 years ago, and in our midst that evening. I think he would say as he did on the cross, in the hands of his enemies: "Father, forgive them; for they know not what they do" (Luke 23:34, KJV). The Good Shepherd still prepares a table for us in the presence of our enemies, so that our eyes would be opened to see and know another way in this world.

Roy Hange spent ten years in Egypt, Syria, and Iran with the Mennonite Central Committee. Adapted from an essay he wrote after the Gulf War, appearing in One World, *June 2001.*

Gifts from Afghan Children

Evelyn Shellenberger

On November 3, 2001, my husband and I visited a camp for displaced Afghans organized by the Iranian Red Crescent Society (IRCS) in a Taliban-controlled section of western Afghanistan.

With a mixture of emotions, we departed Iran to visit one of the refugee camps, called Mile 46. We were accompanied by several IRCS workers who made it easier to pass through the checkpoints. The countryside was desert: flat, dusty, windy. No signs of plant life could be seen.

About four kilometers inside the border, we saw the camp in the distance—rows of tents in neat lines, clouded by dust. Women in the camp were washing clothes, and children were playing in little puddles here and there. The men were busy building bathrooms of clay and brick.

Nearly 600 Afghan refugees are living in the camp, many of whom are children. Each family has access to a tent, blankets, cooking equipment, and food. Huge water tanks are carried in by truck. A generator supplies electricity to the tents. The IRCS staff worry about a prolonged war and the possibility of more refugees. They wonder just how much they can do.

As we walked through the camp, the children told us difficult stories about leaving their homes. They missed their schools, friends, and family. My eye caught sight of a beautiful stone. I stopped and picked it up. Then I saw another and also reached for it. The children watched me carefully. "I want to take these stones back to America with me so I can remember you," I explained. They looked at one another, and smiles crossed their faces.

Later, while in a meeting, I heard a commotion of children's voices outside and went to the door of the tent. There stood a group of about twenty-five children, each holding a beautiful stone. Each child told me his/her name as the gift was given, and I commented on the stone's beauty and value to me. The children told me they had run to the far edges of the camp to find "the best stones."

I have since reflected on this exchange of gifts. Out of compassion we have given of our resources: food, blankets, and money. Out of love, the children have given of their resources: beautiful stones gathered from their land.

May the exchange of life-giving gifts continue as we serve one another.

Evelyn Shellenberger works with the Mennonite Central Committee in Iran.

A Prayer to End the Terror

Lindsay McLaughlin

Creator God,

Heal the broken bodies, hearts, and lives of your children who have suffered in terror and anguish on one of the deadliest days ever on American soil. Help us to dig deep, to the roots of our faith, for sustenance, solace, and wisdom.

The terrorists have offered us a stark view of the world they would create, where the remedy to every human grievance and injustice is to resort to the random and cowardly violence of revenge, even against the most innocent.

Help us to deny the terrorists their victory by refusing to submit to a world created in their image. We must not allow this terror to drive us away from being the people God has called us to be.

Terrorism must end, with terrorists brought to justice. But now we realize that military might, missile defense systems, security checkpoints, and intelligence agencies cannot keep us safe from acts of terror born of hatred. We can kill the terrorists and imprison their accomplices. We can invade and devastate countries that harbor them. But we cannot kill the hatred or destroy the anger.

Give us the courage to stop the terror and violence the only way we can—at its source. We owe it to our children and to the world to look at the roots of the anger that gives rise to terrorism, and to grow, and to change where we must. Give us the courage to call on our leaders to act and lead us in ways truly counter-terrorist—ways of community, compassion, and justice for all the world.

We have seen terrorism now on an unprecedented scale. Our response must also be unprecedented. God heal us. God give us grace. God give us courage. God bless America. God bless the world. Amen.

Lindsay McLaughlin *sees terrorism as a personal issue. Terrorists killed her father in Afghanistan in 1979. Serving as U.S. ambassador in Kabul, he was taken to a hotel room, bound and gagged. A few hours later, he died in a hail of gunfire. He was buried in Arlington Cemetery, near Kennedy's eternal flame. McLaughlin has served as a managing editor at* Sojourners. *She wrote this prayer in response to the September 11 tragedy. Reprinted with permission from* Sojourners, *www.sojo.net. (Telephone 800-717-7474.)*

Questions for Reflection and Discussion

Chapter 1: God Amid the Terror?

1. What questions have you wanted to ask God about the attacks of September 11? Which essays spoke to you? Which answers made the most sense?

2. Several writers mention that God is present with those who suffer and those who serve people in need. In what ways have you experienced this in your own life?

3. Williamson suggests that Psalm 23 affirms God's love and care no matter what happens, but also invites us to eat with our enemies. How do you respond to this interpretation?

4. Several essays suggest that our primary focus should not be on why evil things happen but on how we respond. Do you agree? Why or why not? What are some things we might learn from these events?

Chapter 2: Jesus and the Way of Peace

1. Many of these essays focus on the Sermon on the Mount as a guide for living. How have you applied this sermon to your life? Explain.

2. Several essays argue that Christians should pay more attention to Jesus' teaching about loving our enemies. Do you agree? What changes would this mean for Christians in North America?

3. Several authors suggest that Jesus offered a third way—a more positive, active response to evil—than either passive acceptance or violent force. How can we practice Jesus' way of overcoming evil?

4. How do you understand the Christian claim that Jesus is Lord? To what extent is this true in your own life? How does your allegiance to Jesus apply to your use of violence?

Chapter 3: Revenge, Justice, or Forgiveness?

1. Describe your emotions in the aftermath of the attacks of September 11? What feelings do you have now? What has been helpful in processing your emotions?

2. Several essays note that Jesus and the early church rejected vengeance as an option for Christians. What practical and spiritual dangers might result from violent retaliation?

3. Gross asserts that we are overcome by evil, not when terrible things happen to us, but when we respond to evil with evil. What examples from your own life support this idea? How can we avoid becoming the very evil that we deplore?

4. Volf argues that no one is ever outside the range of God's love. Do you agree? Why or why not?

5. When is forgiveness a sign of weakness and when a sign of strength? When is forgiveness healthy, or unhealthy?

Chapter 4: Will Violence Bring Peace?

1. Do you believe violence is ever necessary? Why are we drawn to the myth that "violence can redeem bad things"? Can you think of examples when violence reduced suffering? When it made things worse?

2. Several writers argue strongly that using violence to counter terrorism will simply breed more terrorism and make us even less secure. Do you agree?

3. Suderman argues that U.S. politicians have used religious language to justify the war against terrorism, making it, in effect, a holy war. Do you think that God "blessed" the war in Afghanistan? How might such claims be dangerous and "use" God for national purposes?

4. Lewis reminds us that violence and terror do not exist only in faraway places. They are also found here at home, in our country. How should the U.S. government address this kind of terror? What should the church be doing?

Chapter 5: Voices from Our Global Family

1. Which voices touched you most deeply? What message(s) did you hear?

2. Many of the letters spoke from their own experience of suffering. What advice and counsel do they give American Christians?

3. Several letters note that the United States sometimes uses its enormous influence in ways that affect people in other countries negatively. How might U.S. Christians demonstrate concern for these brothers and sisters and show our oneness in Christ?

4. Schrag argues that Christians cannot share their faith in Christ and also participate in war. Do you agree?

Chapter 6: Citizens of Two Kingdoms

1. Many writers argue that one's loyalty to God should take precedence over loyalty to nation. When have you experienced a conflict between these loyalties? How did you resolve the dilemma?

2. How can Christians show their love for their country without diluting their allegiance to God's international kingdom? When do you feel comfortable participating in expres-

sions of patriotism? Have you ever had reservations about participating in patriotic events?

3. How do you feel about displaying the flag as an expression of patriotism? Do you think national flags should appear in places of worship? How do you respond to Weaver-Zercher's suggestions?

4. In the story about flags at work, do you agree with how the situation was resolved? What similar situations have you faced? How have you responded?

Chapter 7: Another Way of Responding

1. Which suggestions make the most sense to you? Which suggestions would you urge for the government? Which ones might you consider for yourself or your community?

2. Adeney urges Christians to become more engaged in activities that promote global peace and justice. How do you respond to her suggestions?

3. What might you or your congregation do to relate to Muslims or Arab-Americans in your community?

4. "The Everlasting Supper" is a poignant reminder of how God might bring us face to face with people we considered enemies. What were your feelings as you read this story? Try to imagine a similar situation in your own life. Who might be included? What might you say to one another?

Books

Ackerman, Peter, and Jack Duvall. *A Force More Powerful: A Century of Nonviolent Conflict.* St. Martin's Press, 2001.

Amstutz, Jim S. *Threatened with Resurrection: Self-Preservation and Christ's Way of Peace.* Herald Press, 2002.

Augsburger, Myron S. *The Robe of God: Reconciliation, the Believers' Church Essential.* Herald Press, 2000.

Barrett, Lois. *A Mennonite Statement and Study on Violence.* Herald Press, 1998.

Boulding, Elise. *Cultures of Peace: The Hidden Side of History.* Syracuse University Press, 2000.

Dear, John. *Disarming the Heart: Toward a Vow of Nonviolence.* Herald Press, 1993.

Douglass, James W. *The Nonviolent Coming of God.* Orbis Books, 1991.

Driedger, Lee, and Donald B. Kraybill. *Mennonite Peacemaking: From Quietism to Activism.* Herald Press, 1994.

Friesen, Duane. *Christian Peacemaking and International Conflict.* Herald Press, 1986.

Gish, Arthur. *Hebron Journal: Stories of Nonviolent Peacemaking.* Herald Press, 2001.

Griffith, Lee. *The War on Terrorism and the Terror of God.* Eerdmans, 2001.

Herr, Robert, and Judy Zimmerman Herr, eds. *Transforming Violence: Linking Local and Global Peacemaking.* Herald Press, 1998.

Juhnke, James, and Carol Hunter. *The Missing Peace: The Search for Nonviolent Alternatives in United States History.* Pandora Press, 2001.

Kateregga, Badru, and David W. Shenk. *A Muslim and a Christian in Dialogue*. Herald Press, 1997.

Lederach, John Paul. *The Journey Toward Reconciliation*. Herald Press, 1999.

Nickel, Gordon D. *Peaceable Witness Among Muslims*. Herald Press, 1999.

Shriver, Donald W., Jr. *An Ethic for Enemies: Forgiveness in Politics*. Oxford University Press, 1998 reprint.

Sider, Ron. *Nonviolence: The Invincible Weapon*. Word, 1989.

Stassen, Glen. *Just Peacemaking: Ten Practices for Abolishing War*. Pilgrim Press, 1998.

Tutu, Desmond. *No Future Without Forgiveness*. Doubleday, 1999.

Van Ness, Dan, and Karen Heetderks Strong. *Restoring Justice*. Anderson, 1997.

Volf, Miroslav. *Exclusion and Embrace: A Theological Exploration of Identity, Otherness, and Reconciliation*. Abingdon, 1996.

Wink, Walter. *Engaging the Powers: Discernment and Resistance in a World of Domination*. Fortress, 1992.

Yancey, Philip. *Where Is God When It Hurts?* Zondervan, 2001.

Yoder, John H. *Nevertheless: Varieties of Pacifism*. Herald Press, 1992.

Yoder, John H., with Joan Baez, Tom Skinner, Leo Tolstoy, and others. *What Would You Do* (if a violent person threatened to harm a loved one)? Expanded edition. Herald Press, 1992.

Websites

American Friends Service Committe: www.afsc.org.

Baptist Peace Fellowship of North America: www.bpfna.org.

Beliefnet.com: www.beliefnet.com. Offers resources from many religious traditions. For material on September 11, find the heading, "More recent features" and scroll to "Complete 9/11 coverage."

Brethren in Christ Church: www.bic-church.org.

Centre for Justice and Reconciliation of Prison Fellowship International: www.restorativejustice.org. Offers resources on restorative justice and links to other groups.

Christian Peacemaker Teams: www.prairienet.org/cpt. CPT is a project of Mennonite Churches, the Church of the Brethren, and Friends United Meeting.

Christianity Today: www.christianitytoday.com. For material on September 11, find "Search Hot Topics" and go to "Responding to Terrorism," News and Analysis section.

Church of the Brethren: www.brethren.org. Offers links to denominational programs and peace and justice resources.

Common Dreams: www.commondreams.org. An alternative news source, with links to a wide array of online news sources.

Eastern Mennonite University, Conflict Transformation Program: www.emu.edu. Offers an extensive collection of essays and links to other resources, under the heading, "Beyond September 11: Response by CTP."

Ekklesia Project: www.ekklesiaproject.org. Offers an ecumenical collection of resources and sermons, focusing especially on the tragedy of September 11.

Episcopal Peace Fellowship: www.epfonline.org.

Every Church a Peace Church: www.ecapc.org. Offers written resources as well as links to other groups.

Fellowship of Reconciliation: www.forusa.org. Includes links to other faith-based peace groups.

Friends Committee for National Legislation: www.fcnl.org. Offers resources on a wide array of issues and public policy concerns.

Friends United Meeting: www.fum.org. Offers the Peace Connections Page, the latest *Quaker Life*, and other resources on peace and justice issues.

Lutheran Peace Fellowship: www.lutheranpeace.org.

Mennonite Church Canada: www.mennonitechurch.ca. Includes program updates and peace and justice resources.

Mennonite Church USA: www.mennonitechurchusa.org. Offers program updates and links to denominational peace and justice resources.

Mennonite Central Committee: www.mcc.org. Offers updates on current programs and peace and justice resources.

National Churches of Christ: www.ncccusa.org.

Other Side, The, magazine: www.theotherside.org.

Pax Christi, a national Catholic peace group: www.paxchristiusa.org.

Peace Action, formerly Sane/Freeze: www.peace-action.org. Features an active student network.

Sojourners' magazine: www.sojo.net.

The Editors

Donald B. Kraybill is Professor of Sociology and Anabaptist Studies at Messiah College, Grantham, Pennsylvania, and author of numerous books, such as *The Upside-Down Kingdom* (Herald Press) and *The Riddle of Amish Culture* (The Johns Hopkins University Press). He has served in various leadership roles in the Mennonite Church and the Church of the Brethren.

Don and his wife, Frances, have two daughters and attend the Elizabethtown (Pa.) Church of the Brethren.

Linda Gehman Peachey is a freelance author of Lancaster, Pennsylvania. She wrote the 2001 Mennonite Women Bible Study Guide, "How Then Shall We Live? A Study on the Sermon on the Mount." She has worked with the Lancaster Area Victim Offender Reconciliation Program.

Linda and her husband, Titus, directed Peace and Justice Ministries for Mennonite Central Committee U.S. (1988-96), administered MCC's development aid program in Laos (1981-85), and edited *Seeking Peace* (Good Books), stories of Mennonite peacemakers. They have two daughters and attend East Chestnut Street Mennonite Church in Lancaster.